EARLY TEXAS

ARCHITECTURE

EARLY TEXAS
ARCHITECTURE

by
Gordon Echols

TEXAS CHRISTIAN UNIVERSITY PRESS

Library of Congress Cataloging-in-Publication Data

Echols, Gordon.

Early Texas architecture / by Gordon Echols

    p.cm.

    Includes bibliographical references and index.

    ISBN 0-87565-223-9 (alk. paper)

    ISBN 0-87565-220-4 (pbk. : alk. paper)

1. Regionalism in architecture. 2. Architecture, Modern—
19th century—Texas. 3. Architecture, Modern—20th century—Texas. 4. Architecture—Texas. I. Title.

NA730.T5 E26 2000

720'.9764—dc21

                                 99-055193

Unless otherwise indicated all photographs were taken by
the author; permission has been granted by residents or owners of the structures illustrated.

Cover and text design by Bill Maize—Duo Design Group.

Printed in Canada

To Patton,
a loving wife and mother

Contents

Preface

exas, perhaps more than any other state or geographical area in the United States, developed a distinctive regional architecture. Texas was settled by immigrants from many different backgrounds who modified the construction techniques and styles that they had brought with them, producing a new architecture to fit a land marked by widely varying topography, vegetation and climatic extremes.

This book examines the evolution of early Texas architecture through text and photographs of surviving early buildings that illustrate adaptation to climate, topography and available materials. I have tried to identify cultural influences that contributed to the aesthetic and functional qualities of these structures.

Today much of the regional character of architecture in Texas, as in other parts of the country, has been lost—most new buildings have the look of those everywhere else, and our cities are becoming visually redundant. Only a few surviving landmarks distinguish one region from another. Those structures that remain are significant not only for their aesthetic and historic value, but also for their basic design and construction. Many are still functional and offer lessons for the design of today's built environment.

During six years of research, I examined many original documents, early photographs, plans and drawings. I also gathered information from numerous interviews and site visits. While I could not cover every aspect of early Texas architecture, I have attempted to examine buildings representative of each period and region as extensively as possible. In selecting buildings to include in this book, I considered distinctive architectural details, historical significance and aesthetic merit. My interpretations of the physical and cultural factors behind these structures are based on the best information available, but in many instances it is impossible to verify the "facts." Thus, all interpretation about early architecture must be a synthesis of available data, perceptions of the human eye and analytical and critical capabilities of the human mind. These discussions of the architecture and its evolution are necessarily subjective, and I accept responsibility for any errors in judgment.

No edifice remains exactly as it was the day it was completed: through new uses, improvements, restoration or simply maintenance (or lack of it), changes—whether major or minor—have occurred.

Many individuals and institutions have contributed directly or indirectly to this work. Both the College of Architecture and the Office of University Research at Texas A&M University were particularly supportive of the research for this book and provided several grants for travel and photography. The Texas Committee for the Humanities and the National Endowment for the Humanities provided support for much of my study of Raiford Stripling's restorations. Support for processing and printing photographs was provided by the Texas Commission on the Arts and the National Endowment for the Arts. The Texas Historical Commission generously made available invaluable records necessary for my research. Reproduction of the drawings in the U.S. Department of the Interior's Historic American Buildings Survey was made possible by the assistance of the Center for Historic Resources at Texas A&M University.

The late Raiford Stripling, a San Augustine architect known as the "Dean of Historic Restoration in Texas" and a close friend, introduced me to the surviving works of the highly trained Greek Revival builder Augustus Phelps. I learned much from the hours I spent with Raiford listening to his reminiscences of Texas history and discussions of the social and cultural heritage of early Texas architecture. His extensive work as a restoration architect has established the highest standards for this field and has given me insight. One of the guiding principles which he insisted should be observed in any restoration effort was that "the design of the original building belongs to the original architect or builder and not to a later preservationist. One may take no privileges in altering or modifying in any way a historic building to change the integrity of the original design and construction."

Pamela Puryear of Navasota provided great assistance not only in introducing me to many of Washington County's early buildings, but also in offering historic information and editorial suggestions regarding various drafts of the book.

I express special gratitude to Noel Parsons and Mary Lenn Dixon of Texas A&M University Press and Judy Alter and Tracy Row of Texas Christian University Press for their continual review of the manuscript and their encouragement to complete it.

My sincere appreciation also goes to Alison Tartt for her outstanding efforts and talents in critiquing and editing my writing.

My colleagues in the College of Architecture gave much constructive criticism and encouragement, offering their support when certain unknowns and disappointments connected with the project made its completion seem impossible.

My special indebtedness and thank you are for Wilma Washburn who gave innumerable hours to reading and making valuable suggestions.

The attention and efforts of others who contributed to the research, understanding and development of the project are also acknowledged with deepest appreciation. They include Thomas and Jane Bullock, the late Harvin and wife Elizabeth Moore, Graham Luhn, the late Fr. Benedict Leutenegger, Joe and Martha Freeman, Robert Steinbomer, Caroline Peterson, Dr. Victor Treat, Woodlief Brown, James Rome, Carroll Tharp, Oliver J. Reinhart, Jr., Dorothy Steinbomer Kendall, Ruth Curry Lawler, Fred Pottinger, Tom Messer, Stan Graves, Evelyn Overmiller, Dr. William C. Welch and his wife Diane, Jesus Hinojosa, Dr. David Pugh, Elaine Kowienschke, David Woodcock, Augustus Hamblett, Joan Rabins, Kathi Faust, Dr. Donald Sweeney, Dr. B. J. Adams, and John Boyett.

Early Texas Architecture: An Introduction

Three primary criteria determine the character of early buildings in Texas: geography, availability of construction materials and cultural background of the builder. All early settlers brought with them a knowledge of their traditional building methods and a basic understanding of materials and design to use in adapting to regions where they settled. Texas pioneers from every culture brought tools, hardware and the know-how needed to build homes in the wilderness.

The new life in Texas was primitive and rigorous. In the words of one account, "Here women in drab calico (which sold for 50 cents a yard) stirred 'hog and hominy' with home-made wooden spoons and learned to use the long rifle. They lived in bare, sometimes windowless, log cabins. Flour was $25 a barrel"; it was said that "Texas is a heaven for men and dogs but hell for women and oxen" (Writers' Program of the Works Projects Administration of Texas, *The WPA Guide to Texas*, pp. 38-39). Into this harsh setting the new Texans brought much of their heritage, which influenced the ways that they introduced systematic and practical modifications to their environment. The evolution of their built environment—their architecture—reflected these modifications.

Extremes of climate and topography in the land area encompassed by Texas had a determining influence on the early architecture as settlers adapted materials and construction methods to regional conditions. Between summer and winter temperature extremes are common. Rainfall is also highly variable. Texas is marked by weather that is extreme and often destructive—hurricanes and tropical storms, windstorms and tornadoes, severe thunderstorms, droughts and blizzards. Pioneers learned to take these environmental factors into account and build for survival as well as for comfort. Their architecture was also influenced by the availability of native building materials, which differed considerably from one region to another.

The variability of the physical environment in Texas is due to four natural regions converging within the state's boundaries: Coastal Plains, North Central Plains, Great Plains and Mountains and Basins. These can be further subdivided as:

1. Coastal Plains: Pine Woods; Gulf Coast Plain; South Texas Plain; Post Oak Belt; Blackland Prairie

2. North Central Plains: Grand Prairie; Cross Timbers; Lower Plains

3. Great Plains: High Plains; Edwards Plateau; Llano Basin

4. Mountains and Basins.

The Coastal Plains, which comprise about one-third of Texas, extend from the Gulf of Mexico to the Balcones Fault. The topography along the Gulf and extending inland approximately seventy-five to a hundred miles is relatively flat, with slow-moving streams, bayous and marshes. Westward from the coast, the land becomes higher and more rolling with small hills and valleys. Rainfall varies considerably from an annual average of 20 to 25 inches in the South

Texas Plains to over 55 inches at the Louisiana border. Temperatures range from over 100 degrees to near zero. The vegetation varies considerably according to moisture, drainage, and soil conditions. The loblolly, short leaf and slash pines are prominent in East Texas where soils and rainfall foster their growth. Oak, hickory, gum and cypress traditionally grow in the Post Oak Savannah and farther west. Cypress and pecan exist primarily in more moist soils along streams and overflow areas. Farther to the south and west, where the soil is less fertile and rainfall is sparser, mesquite and other brushy plants are abundant.

The North Central Plains represent the southern extension of the rolling plains of the central United States. This region is bounded by the Red River on the north, the Colorado River on the south, the Cap Rock Escarpment to the west (the delineation line between these plains and the higher Great Plains) and the Balcones Fault and Coastal Plains to the east. Most of the land in this region is rolling, some of it hilly, rocky and rough. Rainfall averages between 20 and 30 inches per year. Temperatures are slightly below those of the Coastal Plains. Vegetation includes post oak, blackjack oak, junipers and

mesquite as well as bunch and short grasses. Most of the soils are rich, supporting cotton and wheat cultivation and providing fine ranchland.

The High Plains, the southern extension of the Great Plains, include most of the Panhandle of Texas south throughout the Edwards Plateau and the Llano Basin or the Hill Country. The northern area of the region is high country (elevations range from 2,500 to 4,000 feet) covered with grasses and mesquite trees. When irrigated, the region provides good farming and ranching. Temperatures range from warm during the summer months to well below freezing in the winter. Rainfall ranges from approximately 15 inches in the west to 20 inches in the east. The region has low humidity and a comfortable climate.

The Mountains and Basins region lies west of the High Plains, primarily west of the Pecos River, and is frequently called the Trans-Pecos. It is generally warm, sunny and dry. Annual rainfall ranges from near zero to approximately 15 inches. Most of the vegetation is desert shrub with some arid-land grasses and with montane forests and oak savannahs at higher elevations. The topography varies from approximately 500 feet above sea level to mountain peaks approaching 9,000 feet. Because of low rainfall, poor soils and

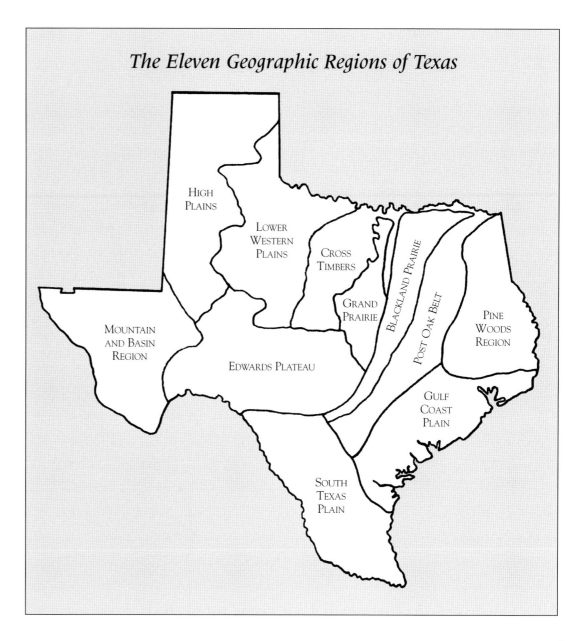

The Eleven Geographic Regions of Texas

HIGH PLAINS

LOWER WESTERN PLAINS

CROSS TIMBERS

BLACKLAND PRAIRIE

GRAND PRAIRIE

POST OAK BELT

PINE WOODS REGION

MOUNTAIN AND BASIN REGION

EDWARDS PLATEAU

GULF COAST PLAIN

SOUTH TEXAS PLAIN

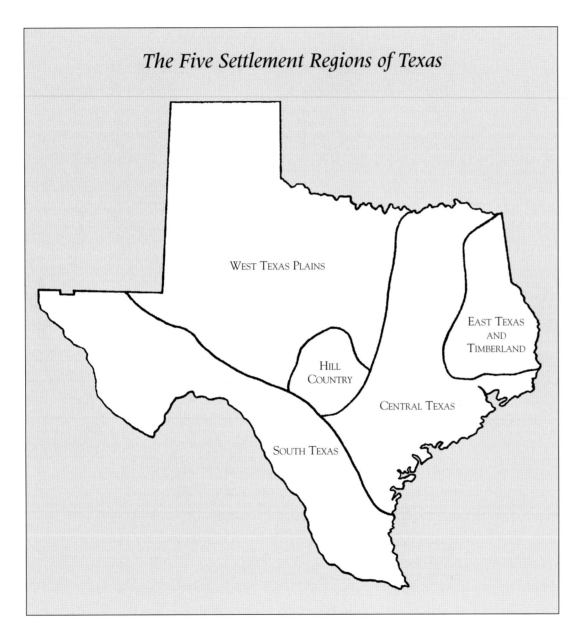

The Five Settlement Regions of Texas

WEST TEXAS PLAINS

EAST TEXAS
AND
TIMBERLAND

HILL
COUNTRY

CENTRAL TEXAS

SOUTH TEXAS

East Texas:
Log construction, later replaced by frame construction.

Central Texas:
Log construction, later replaced by frame and brick.

Hill Country:
Log, adobe or brick construction, quickly replaced by German-style half timber or fachwerk with stone infill.

South Texas:
Spanish/Mexican brush jacals, palisade wall and adobe and stone.

West Texas Plains:
Dugouts and half dugouts, some sod houses, occasional adobe and stone. Most structures were quickly replaved by frame construction.

rugged topography, the area has limited agricultural or ranching use.

For this book, the early architecture will be categorized according to five regions: East Texas Pines and Timberlands, Central Texas Blackland Prairie and Post Oak Savannah, Texas Hill Country, West Texas Plains, and South Texas and the Rio Grande Valley. These five regions are the primary areas of settlement during the years of the Republic and immediately after annexation. Therefore this volume first examines the early Anglo settlements that were established in the far eastern parts of Texas. The narrative then moves west and south.

A number of physical factors—such as water supply, access to transportation and trade and availability of building materials—affected settlement patterns. The Sabine, Trinity, Brazos, Colorado, Guadalupe, San Antonio, San Jacinto, Neches, Nueces and Rio Grande rivers all flow into the Gulf of Mexico from various points north and west. The Red River, the major drainage system in northern Texas, flows into the Mississippi River and historically provided a major transport route from the upper and middle areas of the continent as well as travel and trade from the Gulf of Mexico. The settlers used these rivers for transportation and as a source of water for cattle and irrigation. The alluvial flood plains that adjoin these rivers provided excellent agricultural land for the newcomers.

Settlements also grew up along early Spanish trails and trade routes. The Camino Real, which extended from deep in Mexico and crossed the Rio Grande at Laredo and at San Juan Bautista (near present-day Eagle Pass), linked San Antonio de Bexar with the East Texas missions. Other Spanish trails traversed the region in a northeast-southwest direction to the Sabine River. Major crossroads and watering points often became larger settlements of political, military, economic, governmental, cultural or social importance. Later, cattle trails such as the Chisholm, the Western, and the Goodnight-Loving provided additional stimuli for growth.

Drawing on the technical knowledge they had brought with them, settlers adapted to their new environment using local natural resources. Earth and stone structures had thick walls, which were good insulators and kept the interior cool in summer but warm during the winter. Log structures also provided excellent insulation against extremes of heat and cold. Because of the many individual air cells within the wood, heat and cold transfer from the outside to the inside or vice versa was minimal. In addition to their insulating qualities, log buildings were relatively easy to construct and maintain.

With time, a greater understanding of physical considerations led to habitations that were able not only to withstand the environmental variables but also to contribute to a level of comfort and convenience and to satisfy other human needs, such as for privacy, storage, social exchange, bathing and working, as well as some satisfaction of aesthetics. Houses built on higher ground offered protection from high water and captured cooling summer breezes. Good drainage away from the homestead freed the site from water that collected after a heavy rainfall. Building on an elevated spot not only provided a practical means of overseeing land, livestock, employees and potential visitors but also represented an aesthetic amenity in the form of a good view as well as prestige.

SPANISH COLONIAL [1681-CIRCA 1800]

The first structures in Texas were developed over several generations as Spanish friars, soldiers and, later, settlers from Spain, Mexico and other Spanish colonies penetrated the area. Initially these buildings were temporary and thus made of materials requiring little preparation and only primitive assembly. The earliest form was the jacal, a type of hut likely derived from the native Indian building techniques used throughout this region of the New World. Although the history of the construction method is not fully known, jacals were probably in use before European occupation of the American Southwest. Walls were usually built by setting wood poles into post holes approximately a foot deep and spaced three or four inches to a foot apart. The vertical timbers, somewhat taller than head height and two to six inches in diameter, were laced together with vines or short pieces of pliable sticks and chinked with twigs, small branches and grass; frequently the jacal was plastered over (either outside or inside) with mud. It was not unusual to paint the mud plaster with a white lime wash to give more light to the interior and to offer a finished appearance to the exterior. The common jacal roof was thatch or sacate. Three types of grasses were used: carrizo (reed), sachuiste and sacaton. The framework consisted of a ridgepole supported on each end by *cyucks. Latias*, or rafters, spanned from the ridgepole on each sidewall. The latias were most often the trunks of mesquite trees. The builder determined the approximate length measuring with his axe handle. Often the bark was stripped from the felled mesquite to prevent insect damage. The next step was to lay the *huilotes*, three-to-four-inch wooden strips on top of and perpendicular to the latias. These were tied into place with a thread of pita (agave or maguey cactus fibers). Bundles of grass were then attached to the huilotes, one row at a time. Two men worked together, one on top of the roof and the other underneath. The grass bundles were bound to the huilotes using a wooden needle about six feet long and one inch in diameter and pita threads. The threads were tied off in square knots. By overlapping the successive layers of grass, the roof was made water resistant. The average life of such a roof is said to have been twenty to thirty years. Doors were sometimes of wood but more often, like the windows, of reeds or similar material woven together with hemp or other small vines to allow ventilation and privacy. Floors were simply tamped earth. Because of their simplicity, jacals could be constructed quickly. Originally residences, jacals were especially vulnerable to attack from hostile Indians who used fire as a weapon. As settlements became more permanent, colonists eagerly built houses of stone or adobe with fireproof roofs, and the jacal was relegated to auxiliary uses such as storage or animal shelter. Many of the wood buildings of this period have not survived because of neglect, rot, insect penetration and fire. (For details of jacal construction, see William Clayton Barbee, "A Historical and Architectural Investigation of San Ygnacio, Texas" [master's thesis, University of Texas at Austin, December 1981]).

During the mission period (1632-1821), log and stone buildings were erected, which involved more careful and precise methods. The founding of a mission and its accompanying presidio was seen as a preliminary step toward creating self-sustaining communities, so the mission system promoted the concept of long-term colonies and, with them, more durable buildings. Most of the early Spanish missions were first built of timber or, where wood was scarce, adobe. The earliest mission communities were considered temporary and provided only for the basic needs. They were eventually replaced with buildings made of masonry materials, such as stone and/or plastered brick. The masonry walls of a mission compound and the enclosed buildings were typically three to four feet thick but sometimes as much as eight feet thick.

Mexican Indians, imported to Texas as laborers, were excellent stone masons capable of cutting, placing, mortaring and sculpting limestone. In addition, the local Indians, supervised by friars and in some instances builders from the mother country, were taught such construction techniques as the traditional European arch, vault and buttress or the local post-and-beam framing that allowed simple spans to accommodate the building function. The most decorative architectural details were lavished on the church or chapel, which was the visual focus of the mission complex; it was usually completed after the functional structures had been built. Chapels were frequently constructed first to provide for the liturgical needs of worship; the church, a more formidable structure, was built later to provide more adequately for Christian worship. (See Marion A. Habig, O.F.M., *Spanish Missions of Texas: The Old Franciscan Missions and Other Spanish Settlements of Texas, 1632-1821* [Chicago: Franciscan Herald Press, 1990].)

In addition to the methods of jacal, stone and adobe construction, Spanish colonialists introduced other features suited to the Texas environment, such as vigas and latias, *chipichil*, atria and interior windows. Vigas—roof joists or beams—were placed on bearing masonry or adobe walls at uniform intervals, carefully selected for the span and dead loads needed to support the roof. Latias, small lengths of thinly split wood, were placed over the vigas sometimes positioned perpendicularly but more often arranged in a diagonal pattern, thus creating a basket-weave pattern in the ceiling. A matrix of lime and small, pea-sized crushed stone aggregate was mixed with water to form a mudlike paste and was placed over this supporting surface. When cured this material—which insulated and shed rain—was known as chipichil and resembled plaster. The traditional roof construction was nearly flat with only enough slope to drain off rainwater and discharge it below the masonry parapet walls through *canales*.

Because this type of roof created a rather heavy load, the supporting walls were of load-bearing materials, most commonly adobe and sometimes stone or brick. Load-bearing masonry walls had a thickness of from two to four feet, so windows and doors were recessed—either to the exterior or interior—which provided deep window sills and door jambs.

PIONEER SETTLEMENT {1820-1870}

In the nineteenth century, as colonization in Texas became more widespread and more representative of a variety of ethnic groups, buildings became more individual in character, with cultural traditions and environmental factors combining to produce an architecture with distinct regional features. The building materials were predominantly wood, stone and earth, but these basic materials were applied in different ways. Earth, for instance, could be used for a sod house or an adobe house or as the chinking in a log house.

In the northern and western parts of Texas, for example, building materials were limited to earth and stone. Here on the plains and prairies, the buildings were typically sod houses, dugouts, half-dugouts and structures of adobe and stone. In the Rio Grande Valley and other parts of South Texas, stone and earth were the most available native materials, although some temporary structures—like palisade and jacal forms—made use of branches and brush. Trees of significant scale and quantity were abundant in East Texas, so early settlers in this region enjoyed a distinct advantage with respect to construction.

Log construction—brought to the region by pioneers from Georgia, Tennessee, Kentucky, Virginia, the Carolinas and Missouri, as well as by German immigrants—is the predominant indigenous architecture of Texas and probably represents the purest form of regional architecture. The extent of its use depended on the availability of trees of adequate size, but it could be adapted easily to various areas and was a highly practical building technique, well suited for the primitive, labor-intensive technology of the time. There is speculation that some American Indians or Anglo adventurers in Texas may have used log techniques as early as the 1790s. The earliest evidence of log construction by Anglo-Americans in Texas dates to the period 1812-1825 (see Terry G. Jordan, *Texas Log Buildings* [Austin: University of Texas Press, 1978], p. 27).

German immigrants introduced the *fachwerk* framed structure, usually infilled with stone, brick or adobe.

Earth and log construction yielded to frame as soon as timber could be imported. Many of the stone structures were retained as bunkhouses or storage facilities while the less permanent sod houses and dugouts were frequently abandoned and allowed to decompose.

In the Rio Grande Valley and other parts of South Texas, vegetation consisted primarily of mesquite, brush and desert srub. Stone and earth were the most available native materials.

In East Texas, trees of significant scale and quantity were abundant, giving early settlers a distinct advantage in construction. Fully mature forests of pine, oak, pecan, hickory, cypress, gum, elm, bois d'arc and cedar provided an almost unlimited supply of high quality heartwood. The tall, straight longleaf pines were especially advantageous for producing logs and sawn timber.

GREEK REVIVAL
[1838-1870]

In 1838, with the arrival in San Augustine of the builder Augustus Phelps, Greek Revival architecture was introduced to Texas. Phelps probably came from New England and was trained in the Greek Revival style in Philadelphia. He contracted to build five houses within a two-year period in San Augustine, apparently using designs found in popular books of the time, including John Haviland's *The Builder's Assistant* (1818), Asher Benjamin's *The Practice of Architecture* (1833) and Minard LaFever's *The*

Beauties of Modern Architecture (1835). Abner Cook, who designed and built the Governor's Mansion in Austin in 1855, was another leading builder in Texas and a master of the Greek Revival style.

The Greek Revival style had become popular in the United States during the second quarter of the nineteenth century after Thomas Jefferson had introduced the Classic Revival (Roman) style with the design and construction of Virginia's capitol building in Richmond and the University of Virginia (1785-1788). The outbreak of the Greek war for independence in 1821 fueled the popularity of the Greek Revival style—Americans, particularly Texans, saw the style as a symbol of democracy and self-rule. Public support for the Greeks was so great, in fact, that many American towns—Athens, Corinth, Troy, Sparta and Syracuse, for example—were named or renamed in the period.

In Texas, Greek Revival architecture was especially favored by Anglo-Americans who had migrated from the southeastern states where the style flourished. It was particularly appropriate to the hot, semitropical climate of certain parts of Texas. The form of the Greek temple provided the basic shape of the building, which was usually two stories with a symmetrical floor plan around a central wide hallway. This wide central hall with double doors at the front and the back of the passage provided through ventilation. An equal number of parlors and other rooms were located on either side of the central axis, which also improved air circulation, as did the tall windows and louvered shutters. High ceilings and an attic accommodated the intense heat of the region, and the colonnaded verandah and a pedimented portico on one or more sides of the building provided shade.

The Greek Revival period ended soon after the Civil War, but provided one of the most popular architectural styles, not simply in Texas but throughout the nation. Many attractive buildings in that style survive today. Some of the finest examples were the residences of prosperous East Texas cotton farmers who could afford to hire master builders and craftsmen from the East.

VICTORIAN
[1870-1917]

Victorian architecture perhaps least reflects a decidedly Texan form of architecture. Although the style was introduced to Texas from other areas of the nation, it became a dominant part of the state's architectural heritage after the mid-nineteenth century. In fact, Victorian architecture evolved as a result of external forces—a multitude of products and production processes that were made possible by the advances of the Industrial Revolution—rather than any regional or cultural factors. Expanded transportation facilities made a broader selection of materials and technology available. Consequently, the Victorian style was modified very little for specific geographic areas, although in Texas it produced a vernacular architecture with numerous variations, including Second Empire, Stick, Queen Anne, Shingle, Richardsonian Romanesque, Eastlake and Folk Victorian.

The rise of the Victorian style coincides with the new wealth that emerged after Reconstruction through cotton farming, cattle ranching, the railroad industry and the early petroleum industry. Wealthy families built large homes as an expression of their economic position, and Victorian mansions appeared in major cities and small towns alike. These buildings were built primarily of wood frame, brick and some stone masonry. Wood-frame houses were frequently painted white; however, the use of multiple colors was not unusual. Often the trim was painted a darker shade or more animated color than the siding, using grays, blues, browns and yellows. Brick masonry was regularly embellished with carefully laid patterns, ledges, and joints, sometimes incorporating glazed polychrome tile.

Some of the unique features of Victorian architecture, such as extended porches and verandas, large window transoms over doors, raised ceilings and raised pier foundations, were particularly well suited to the Texas climate. High ceilings and large attic spaces provided for air movement and heat dissipation. Large, high windows allowed for ventilation, and open foyers, hallways and stairs facilitated air circulation. Shuttered windows restricted sun glare and radiation, and deep porches and porticos with gingerbread and lattice work shaded the walks and openings to the outside.

The Victorian style abandoned the symmetrical plan and façade of Greek Revival and pioneer houses and introduced embellishments in form and mass as well as ornamentation of detail. Turrets, large bay windows, complex roof forms and gables, dormers, elaborate chimneys, porches and stairs all created an expression of affluence.

Ornamental detail was provided by ornate gingerbread porches, balusters, columns, column capitols, pilasters, porticos, roof ornaments, window sashes and frames, shingles, tiles, masonry, lattice, doors and shutters. The production of the intricate wood ornamentation so typical of the Victorian era was made possible by the jigsaw, lathe and other sophisticated tools of the time. These embellishments in wood and cast iron were produced in millwork production centers in St. Louis and other towns throughout the Midwest and shipped to Texas via the Mississippi River, the Red River or through the ports of Galveston and Beaumont. Then they were moved overland by wagon and rail to the building sites.

Through generations of gradual change and development, Texas architecture synthesized function, mass, space, scale, structure and construction into an architectural expression of the cultural legacy and environmental transformations of its occupants.

* * *

There are approximately 3000 historic buildings in Texas, either on the "National Register of Historic Places" or eligible to be on the registry. During the search for examples of early Texas architecture for this volume, the author was necessarily selective in attempting to locate important structures and in trying to identify examples of excellence in design. The selections included are only a small sample. Many of these buildings have been or are being preserved and restored and will remain a legacy to the pioneer settlers, the architects and the builders. It is the responsibility of both public and private individuals and organizations to continue this meaningful enterprise.

The scope of this volume does not include Native American structures, and—for the most part—churches, missions, military establishments and government and public buildings. That would require a separate book in itself.

ONE

EAST TEXAS
PINES AND TIMBERLAND

East Texas is the region first settled by Anglo-Americans and Afro-Americans, both groups from the southern United States. After the 1803 Louisiana Purchase, it was easiest for migrants to travel overland from Louisiana to Texas. Many individuals and families floated down the Mississippi River to the Red River, then up the Red through Louisiana to Texas. Others traveled the Natchez Trace from Nashville and other points in Tennessee or Mississippi to Natchez; some floated the Mississippi River to New Orleans and across the Gulf of Mexico; some came across Louisiana to Natchitoches, then into Texas on the Camino Real.

Many of the early settlers came from desperate financial, social or legal situations. They were in search of new homes: land, a roof over their heads, water, a modest means of subsistence and an opportunity to begin a new life. The provisions of the land grants to Moses and Stephen F. Austin offered settlers substantial land rewards for migration and settlement with the potential for livelihood in the grant areas. Texians, those who had taken part in the Texas Revolution, were given large land grants contingent on participation in battle or simply serving in the volunteer army. Some early settlers decided not to stay and traded their land grants to others, thereby allowing a few settlers to accumulate larger parcels. Some of the descendants of these pioneers have enjoyed the legacies of their ancestors through the economic benefits of agriculture, cattle, oil and mineral deposits and real estate.

Large previously primeval forests produced millions of board feet of heart pine, cedar, and cypress, the major building materials in the region at the time. Today, the vast pine second growth supplies the building industry with timber, plywood, particle board, wood mulch and other processed forest products. Agricultural production consists primarily of cotton, livestock and cattle, dairy products, poultry, rice, vegetables and small grains.

Mean annual temperature in East Texas ranges from 66 to 70 degrees Fahrenheit, with highest and lowest recorded extremes ranging from 5 degrees to 108. Mean annual precipitation ranges from 44 to 56 inches per year. Mean annual relative humidity ranges from 55 to 90 percent, and mean annual possible sunshine ranges from 65 to 70 percent of the daylight hours. Severe weather has tested the soundness and design of the buildings, compelling builders to develop responsible architecture and construct solid homes suited to the region.

The Greek Revival Houses of San Augustine

(East Texas Pines and Timberland)

Master builder Augustus Phelps came to San Augustine in 1838, two years after the Texas Revolution, and introduced to Texas the first examples of Greek Revival architecture, then popular on the East Coast. Most Texas immigrants during this era came from the southern states, where the Greek Revival style had been introduced by Thomas Jefferson and developed as the vernacular of the late 1820s, continuing as a popular design until the Civil War. The Jeffersonian classical architecture, derived from the Roman orders, was prominent during the second quarter of the nineteenth century as a prelude to this significant period in American design. Incorporating Palladian detail (Andrea Palladio's *Four Books of Architecture*, Leoni's edition of 1715 or 1742 or both), Jefferson's style adapted the Roman temple to a form appropriate to the democracy of the new nation. The inspiration of the Greek democracy, representing freedom, beauty and grandeur, was also adapted to the needs of the new republic. (For details on Jefferson's influence see Talbot Hamlin, *Greek Revival Architecture in America* [New York: Dover Publications, reproduction of the work first published by the Oxford University press, 1944, p. 86] and Fisk Kimball, *Thomas Jefferson, Architect* [Cambridge: Riverside Press, 1916], p. 87.)

Augustus Phelps probably came from New England, likely undertook his builder's apprenticeship in Philadelphia and was likely also trained as an attorney. He migrated to Texas at the age of twenty-eight as a young builder, knowledgeable of the Greek orders. In all likelihood, he had copies of the handbooks for carpenters and builders, including Minard Lefever's *The Beauties of Modern Architecture* (1835); *The Modern Builder's Guide* and *The Practical House Carpenter* (1830); Owen Biddle's *Young Carpenter's Assistant* and Asher Benjamin's *The Practice of Architecture* (1833), *The Practical House Carpenter*, and *The Builder's Guide*. These were the major sources for detailed drawings, dimensions and descriptions of classical orders. Phelps had good knowledge of these details, as well as an ability to apply their principles to the proportions, balance, forms and symmetry of the buildings. This style helped to stimulate an appreciation for beauty and the arts that Texas had not previously encountered.

At the time Phelps arrived, there was little affluence in Texas among the Anglo-American settlers. A very few brought some limited wealth with them in addition to their personal belongings, however. But as more settlers came to Texas from the southern states, they introduced an appreciation for the fine classical revival houses they had seen in their communities back home, promoting the style until it quickly became popular in Texas.

Most of the San Augustine houses were modest in scale; however, Phelps gave them visual sophistication with beauty and dignity. The use of fluting on the Doric columns, the Doric capitals, the columnar entasis, the use of elliptical or semicircular fanlights, sidelights and transom lights around the front door, classical moldings on the cornice, the dentils below and the pedimented porticos were products of his architectural genius.

San Augustine is in far eastern Texas, at the northeastern extreme of the Camino Real, a stopping-off point and trading post for people coming into and leaving the region. Because of this strategic location, the community extracted money from overland immigrants and those settlers who, fostered by astute merchants, were willing to trade currency or land scrip for commodities.

The first water-powered sawmill in the San Augustine area was built in 1837 on the Ayish Bayou. The town's location on a major road and this innovation for sawing timber in all likelihood are the determinants that brought Phelps to San Augustine.

Three examples of Greek Revival houses that Phelps designed and constructed survive in San Augustine: the Ezekiel Cullen House, the Matthew Cartwright House and the Stephen W. Blount House, all executed in 1839. The energy and ingenuity that went into these buildings at this primitive period of architectural development in Texas was indeed a significant accomplishment. It is thought that Phelps had sophisticated hand tools for the day: planes with many specially shaped and ground cutting blades for classical molding configurations including fluted columns; flat hand planes to surface pit sawn, circular sawn and split timber boards; chisels and mallets, perhaps a mule powered lathe, metal-working tools, punches, shears and forges. It is also surmised that he brought with him two servants who were skilled in the building craft.

After the timber was rough sawn at the Ayish Bayou mill, all planks and trim were then hand planed. All Greek details, including cornices, molds, architraves, flutes and dentils, all windows including sills, mullions, muttons, sashes, stops, jambs, all doors including stiles, heads, frames, panels and threshes were cut, planed and assembled. Wood gutters were rough sawn, then hand planed with blades ground especially to shape the concave troughs and the convex exterior molding.

Wooden Doric capitals and round medallion ornaments attached to the top corners of the intersection of the head and jambs of the doorframe were turned on a mule-powered lathe. The Doric columns were cut from cedar or cypress logs by splitting and shaping longitudinal pie-shaped sections, then hand planing the flutes into the exterior radial surface, simultaneously tapering a slight curve from bottom to top to create the entasis of the column. The sections were then individually matched, fitted and nailed together with care so that no joints or nail heads were visible. The last section was fitted into the cylinder and re-nailed in place, the nails counter sunk and the nail holes filled carefully.

Blue marl, another excellent building material because of its softness when first quarried, is a local sedimentary stone taken from shallow deposits in the area. It can be sawed, broken and chiseled with relative ease when first removed from the earth. After its exposure to air for several days, the outer surface begins to oxidize, becomes tempered with a hard exterior casing and the off-white-to-blue color changes to a deep rust red. Marl is used extensively for foundations, chimneys and paving.

Phelps' metal work was used primarily for the construction of leader heads, the metal boxes located at the upper corners of the house to collect rainwater from the wood gutters. He designed and constructed these with an artist's sophistication, always using the Lone Star as the symbolic monogram. Down spouts, discharging the water from the leader heads, were likewise shaped from sheet iron. Square cut nails were fashioned from sheet iron to the length and width required.

THE MILTON GARRETT HOUSE

San Augustine County

In 1826, Milton Garrett, the son of Jacob Garrett who had received a large land grant from Mexico, built the oldest surviving house in San Augustine County. Milton Garrett was appointed by the Mexican government as alcalde—judicial officer or senior judge—for the grant. His log house is one of the few restored to its original state and is an excellent example of domestic design and construction of the pre-Republic period.

The Garrett house is purposely located on a high, well-drained elevation, with exposure to the cooling breezes, an excellent view in all directions; it faces the Camino Real. Near the house is a large, continuously flowing spring, thought to have been a site of Indian occupation.

The heart-pine logs used in this house were cut from mature trees from the local virgin forests. These native pines had very thin layers of sap wood, making it possible to harvest trees, remove the outer layer and leave large heartwood logs for construction. Pine heartwood, often referred to as the "fat," contains a high accumulation of toxic chemicals, providing a wood resistant to rot, termite penetration and other wood-eating insects. These chemicals account for the long life of buildings constructed during the early settlement of Texas. This pine is different from the timber of the second- and third-generation trees cut today that lack the large volume of heart-wood found in the old trees. On the other hand, a distinct disadvantage to heart-pine trees was the flammability of the saps and the desiccated wood fibers caused by the process of air drying over extended time. Many fine buildings of the past have been lost to fire.

In the Garrett house, hand-hewn heart-pine logs enclose two rooms on the ground floor and one large loft on the second floor. The lower rooms were used primarily for living

THE MILTON GARRETT HOUSE *continued*

and sleeping while the loft was for the use of the boys in the family. The horizontal siding, applied over the log construction beneath the porch and gable ends of the "salt box" to the back, is hand-planed stock from local heart pine.

The two chimneys are of blue marl stone. The fireplaces and hearths are constructed inside the house, while the chimneys are erected on the outside. As the flues extend upward, the stone is laid an inch or more away from the log wall, separating the chimney from the house and providing minimum water penetration between the materials to avoid wood rot.

The doors and windows exhibit an exceptional accuracy of workmanship and detail. There are no fillers, shims, or glues, only closely fitted cut and hand-planed wood pieces.

Lapped splice joint

Decorative elements of the house were worked out as part of the assembly. The nailing pattern, securing the vertical and horizontal boards to the door and shutters, is precisely ordered for symmetry, expressing the carpenter's design.

The square capital and corner-edged column of the porch posts supporting the beams show an aesthetic sense. The lapped splice joint of the beam above the post is a structural as well as a visual design element, articulating simplicity. The cedar railing provides a sensitive scale and rhythm.

The half-dovetail joint is one of the more commonly used for log construction in Texas. Using traditional skills, the timber was first harvested, frequently using a two-man crosscut saw and an ax to fell the tree and remove the branches. A crosscut saw was often used to cut the tree trunk to length and to square the ends; a carpenter's adz was used to hew flat surfaces on the outside and inside faces of the logs. Though there were many round-log structures built for housing animals and storing goods, it was important to face the logs for a residence; a flat surface on the exterior walls sheds rainwater effectively, allowing less penetration and less possibility of rot. A flat surface on the interior walls offers an acceptable surface, both functionally and visually.

The half-dovetail log joint was prepared with a handsaw, sawing the notch across the grain. Then an ax was used to split the log along the grain to remove excess material. Each joint was specifically tailored to fit the matching log, maximizing the close fit and minimizing water penetration and standing. The half dovetail allowed water to drain from the joint by gravity, reducing the possibility of wood rot.

The wood-shake roof, although not original to the house, uses reproductions of identical hand-split shakes, cut, split, planed and fitted with an overlap to minimize water penetration. The original shakes were likely split with a broad ax and tapered on the underside with a drawknife, giving a rough, undulating surface and allowing adequate air circulation between each shake that permitted the wood to dry quickly after a rain.

The late Raiford Stripling, architect, bought this house from a direct descendent of Milton Garrett, restored it and maintained it as his residence for many years.

COLONEL STEPHEN WILLIAM BLOUNT HOUSE

San Augustine, San Augustine County

The Stephen W. Blount house, built by Augustus Phelps in 1839 and restored by Stripling as his family home and later willed to his son Ragland "Raggy" and family, is one of the finest examples of Greek Revival architecture in Texas. The house is delicate in scale, in sympathy with the austerity of the days of the Republic and is finely proportioned as a simple Greek temple form. The projection of the entablature and the portico, supported by the fluted columns and Doric capitals, accents the main entrance and emphasizes the symmetrical face. The paneled front door is delineated by pilasters on each side and a half-circle transom window above. A Roman icon completes the articulation of the front entrance. The frieze is developed with the traditional details taken from the Doric order. (See the glossary for descriptions of the triglyph, metope,

The trim above the window heads and outside the jambs was hand-planed and fitted to the corner pieces to complete the window articulation.

The sheet-metal leader heads are a unique architectural semblance not related to the Greek details of the building. The embellishment of the stars across the top and the large star in the center are a Phelps statement that this is a Texas house.

tenia, gutjae and regula.) The rectangular pilasters with the Doric capitals at the corners of the building accent the termination of each wall, introducing the right angle corners. The gabled end walls are completed with a cornice, pediment, and frieze.

Each piece of applied wood, including the individual dentils, was precisely hand shaped, fitted, nailed into place with tiny square-cut nails, and countersunk to provide a monolithic appearance as though the composite elements had been cut from one single piece of material.

MATTHEW CARTWRIGHT HOUSE

San Augustine, San Augustine County, 1839

The Matthew Cartwright house was built in 1839 by Augustus Phelps for Isaac Campbell, who left San Augustine shortly after its completion. The house was used temporarily by the newly formed Wesleyan College for classroom space until Tennessee-born Matthew Cartwright bought it in 1847. Cartwright had three stores in San Augustine on which he built a sizeable estate both in land and commerce. (At the time of his death

Cartwright had bartered for or had bought a million acres of Texas property. See *The New Handbook of Texas* [Austin: Texas State Historical Association, 1996], vol. 1, p. 1004.)

The house again illustrates Phelps' interpretive genius in the use of the refinements of Greek Revival architecture. It is a classic example of the temple form with visually pleasant proportions of façade design, fenestration and detail. The symmetry is articulated by the front portico, supported by two Doric fluted columns with capitals and pilasters on either side of the door. The equidistant symetrical window placement around the portico and front door contributes to the design, each window presenting a six-over-six sash. Greek details are prominent in the entablature at the gabled ends with the molding at the cornices below the eaves and at the frieze.

An adjacent smaller building that closely follows the Greek design and details of the larger house served as an office.

EZEKIEL CULLEN HOUSE

San Augustine, San Augustine County

In 1839 Augustus Phelps completed the Ezekiel Cullen House. Raiford Stripling restored it in 1952 for Hugh Roy Cullen, grandson of Ezekiel. In 1953, the house was given to the Ezekiel Cullen Chapter of the Daughters of the Republic of Texas. The chapter has carefully maintained the house, furnishing it with period pieces and using it as a repository of local historic artifacts.

Even though it has been added to over the years, the house maintains the beauty and scale of the original domestic function. It is well proportioned according to the standards of Greek Revival form, dimension and detail. Four fluted Doric columns—traditionally not placed on a base as are Ionic and Corinthian columns and capitals—with entasis and capitals symmetrically support the porch and entablature. The double front door and the four windows on the front wall are likewise symmetrically located, completing the total composite of the façade. An elliptical operating fan window, with two

EZEKIEL CULLEN HOUSE *continued*

symmetrical operating sliding units, is located in the center of the pediment. That window and a duplicate on the reverse face of the house gives a Greek appointment to both front and back, providing cross ventilation for the second floor. Ventilation in Texas is meaningful during the warm months and was especially necessary to the garret, originally used as a ballroom and for other social entertainment.

Phelps' trademark Lone Star is centered over the double front door. Hand-planed pilasters at each jamb with the traditional plinth at the base surround the door and windows. Each head is trimmed with the identical molding.

On the east and west faces of the porch, Phelps introduced a precisely cut and fitted sun-shading trellis. The heart-pine components are approximately three-quarters of an inch thick with a width of approximately two-and-one-half inches. Each joint is carefully notched in mirror image, so that when joined, the pieces close precisely with the others, creating a multiple of diamond shapes.

The moldings applied to the pediment likewise are hand-planed and fitted precisely as if extruded by modern manufacturing process. The depth of the pediment fascia, continuing around the entire house, provides a sharp contrast between the white house and the dark shadow.

The metal leader heads are similar to those used on the Blount house.

Phelps' interior work was crafted with a sophistication equal to that of the exterior. Door and window surrounds are trimmed with classic wood molding, also hand-planed from the local heart-pine timber. A particular trademark of his work was the five-panel door, a preference Stripling believed was another Phelps symbol of the five-pointed star of Texas. Whatever Phelps' interest in the configuration, each door is designed and constructed with precision. The top three horizontal panels graduate in declining scale, while the two bottom panels are identical and symmetrically placed in the door. All panels are carefully fitted with a surround of classic molding. The five-panel door is not an unusual design in nineteenth-century carpenter houses.

The wainscoting, including the paneling below and the baseboard, are all detailed with classic molds and precisely fitted as though cast as a monolithic piece.

HALF-WAY INN

Nacogdoches County

Half-Way Inn was built before 1837 as a stagecoach stop one days' trip—or halfway—between San Augustine and Nacogdoches. Hence the name. It is thought that such important persons as Sam Houston, Robert E. Lee, and Stephen Austin stayed in the house.

At one time, symmetrical wings extended in either direction from the sides of the house and square columns supported the porch roof. The primary structure is constructed from cedar logs and covered with siding and with board and batten. The plan features the traditional central hall, with stairs and similar rooms symmetrically located on either side.

The windows are balanced around the double front door and are patterned as nine-over-nine panes. The chimneys are of plaster over stone. The form is quite simple and the embellishments are austere. Likely it was a most attractive building in its time.

During the late 1980s, the building was moved from its original site to one closer to Nacogdoches to be restored and returned to service. After the move, Raiford Stripling fondly referred to it as the "three-quarter way house." At the time of this writing the components remain disassembled and have deteriorated from exposure to the elements.

HORN-POLK HOUSE

San Augustine, San Augustine County

The Horn-Polk House was built in 1840 by brothers, Ranson H. and F. N. Horn. After Augustus Phelps' premature death at the age of twenty-eight or twenty-nine from pneumonia (probably contracted on the way to Austin to build the first state capitol), F. N. Horn, a cabinet and furniture maker, bought Phelps' tools and developed his own trade as a carpenter.

Some Greek Revival characteristics are incorporated in this house, though not to the extent or the sophistication of buildings of the well-trained and talented Phelps. The symmetry around the front entrance and the pleasant proportions of the front of the house are among its fine features. The side-window lights at the entrance and the transom light above the double door within a protected cover give an inviting aspect to the house. The hand-planed moldings around the double front doors, the sidelights and the transom offer a delineation of elements. The plinth at the base of the front door pilasters offers a pleasing visual appeal. The carved shell above the transom light over the front doors is unique to this particular house.

CHRIST CHURCH, 1848, 1870

San Augustine, San Augustine County

Christ Church, the "mother church," of the first Episcopal parish in Texas, was established in 1848 by the Reverend Henry Sanson. The original brick building collapsed during a heavy storm due to faulty construction. The present structure was completed in 1870. The box-and-strip (or board-and-batten) siding is constructed of one-and-a-quarter-inch heart-pine lumber. The roof is supported by wood trusses and covered with wood shingles. The corners are reinforced with wrap-around boards to give structural strength as well as offer visual enunciation of the design.

This Gothic building was designed and constructed with the intent of providing vertical empathy with the viewer through the collective elements. The steep roofs on the main building—particularly the bell tower—the lancet-arch windows and the vertical texture of the battens on the exterior walls all contribute to accent the upward emphasis. The simple Gothic forms expressed by the bell tower and its steep roofs add to the liturgical spirit.

The outlookers, under the gable overhangs, serve as support members for the fascia board and the soffit. The order of uniform spacing of these elements gives a sense of honesty to the construction and a visual integrity to the details. Under the eaves at the sidewalls a series of soffit supports are fastened into the roof truss system and extended to carry the overhang. The rhythm of the spacing and the round configuration at the ends of the support members gives an artistic embellishment to the roof and wall intersections.

As in most early Texas architecture, the simple forms compose a modest building mass.

The building was restored by Raiford Stripling.

Jefferson, Texas, Marion County

North of San Augustine, Jefferson is the site of a number of historic structures dating to the mid-nineteenth century. In the late 1840s Jefferson had emerged as a leading commercial and distribution center and the state's leading inland port. With the decline of steamboat traffic and the coming of the railroads the town lost its prominence. In 1971, however, a major section of the city containing fifty-six historic structures was accorded National Register status. Today, Jefferson is experiencing an economic and cultural revival, welcoming people from afar to a city boasting a wealth of historic structures, charming overnight accommodations and restaurants (see, *The New Handbook of Texas*, vol. 3, pp. 924-25).

FREEMAN PLANTATION

Jefferson, Marion County

This Greek Revival house with Louisiana influences was built by William Freeman in 1850 of heart pine, cypress, and handmade clay brick on a thousand-acre cotton and sugar plantation. The plantation was located near the early steamboat port, making available easy movement of goods produced on the plantation and easy import of outside commodities.

The house sits on a rise, giving it good drainage, ventilation and a view. The first-level walls are constructed of brick as is the ground-level floor. The second level is wood, adhering to the Louisiana and East Texas architectural concept of the "raised cottage," a concept developed in these damp locations to allow less moisture to penetrate the structure and the principal living areas.

The scale and proportions of the house and the Greek details are particularly attractive. The plan is traditionally symmetrical with rooms of similar scale on either side of the large central halls on both levels. The hall was important as a receiving room and living space, as well as for providing through ventilation.

The form is a simple rectangular cube, with a front veranda supported by four plain, symmetrically located two-story columns without capitals but with obvious entasis around the front door. The double front door is traditional Greek detail with transom light and two sidelights. The tall windows with six-over-six panes in each are symmetrically located around the house. The exterior porch stairs and banisters are compatible with the façade of the building. The entablature is gracefully developed with moldings derived from the Greek form and accentuated by the corner pilasters that include small Doric capitals.

THE PRESBYTERIAN MANSE {GENERAL JAMES HARRISON ROGERS HOUSE}

Jefferson, Marion County

This classic house is the finest example of Greek Revival architecture in Jefferson. Some reports date the construction as 1839 or 1840; however, the most reliable date is probably 1853.

Built by Charles G. Peel as his family residence, the one-story frame house covered by clapboard is elevated above ground level on a brick foundation wall. The property was sold to General James Rogers in 1856 and acquired by the Presbyterian Church about 1880. Today it is privately held but still referred to as "The Manse."

The plan of the house is traditional with a ten-to-ten-and-a-half-foot-wide central hall, large double doors at either end that provide ventilation and two major rooms on either side. The form of the building is simple: a rectangular solid with hipped roof over the enclosed portion of the house and hipped extensions over each of the two porticos. Sited on a corner property, "The Manse" was constructed with a tetrastyle portico on the two street sides, accenting the main and secondary entrances. Sometime after 1938, a hexastyle portico was added to the back of the house. A full entablature extends around the entire house, supported at the two porticos by fluted, Doric columns with carefully proportioned entasis. At the juncture of the porticos to the house, rectangular section pilasters with square Doric capitols accent the rhythmic details.

Though there is no indication that architectural pattern books of the period were consulted for the design and construction of this house, its sophisticated classic details are outstanding. (See Benjamin, *The Practice of Architecture*, Lafever, *The Beauties of Modern Architecture* and Biddle, *Young Carpenter's. . . .*)

The double front door, with sidelights on either side and a transom light above, allows natural light in the hall, while the portico roof shades the glass from the strong summer sun. The symmetry of the fenestration is carefully delineated with equally spaced windows on either side of the portico.

"The Manse" is truly an outstanding example of Greek Revival architecture and one of the finer works of this period in Texas.

THE FRENCH HOUSE

Jefferson, Marion County

Completed in 1861, this dwelling was probably constructed for a French doctor. Manufacturers' stamps on the windows, doors and interior shutters indicate that they were produced in France. The materials were probably shipped to New Orleans and then sent by river to Jefferson. The house exhibits a distinctive French Gothic Revival or a country influence from northern France that is unusual for northeastern Texas.

The plan of this single-story house modifies the central hall with two similar large rooms on either side. The dining room, an expansion of the far end of the hall, is joined with two rooms on either side. Probably during the early 1900s, a small screened porch was added to the back; it is now enclosed. To control cooking odors, fires and heat gain, the original kitchen was separated from the main house by a breezeway, a common practice of the day.

The massing of the house—accented by the portico—is symmetrical with the hall as the axis of the form. The two attached parlor rooms are clearly delineated by parallel, steeply gabled roofs on either side joined at right angles to the roof over the central hall.

The house sits on brick piers on level grade and is con- structed of wood frame and covered with clapboard. Four square columns placed on pedestals, each with classic Doric square capitals, support the flat-roofed portico with its entabla- ture, cornice, frieze and architrave. Similar pilasters at the juncture of the roof to the house accent the symmetrical arrangement of the vertical forms. Double doors, surrounded by sidelights and a transom light, highlight the front entrance. These French doors are composed of three panels each, the top ones having a semicircular head, the center one a circular con- figuration.

The windows are fourteen-feet high and narrow with wood double-hung sashes and four-over-four panes. Each win- dow is protected from the sun by interior bifold louvered shut- ters. Those on the front and back of the house are covered by an eared Gothic molding at the head; those on the sides feature French Gothic crossettes at the head.

The gables are cased with ornate fascia, verge or barge boards each with a teardrop loop on the lower terminus. The apex of the gable fascia is joined by a carpenter Gothic detail. The ridges are covered by the original metal dragon tooth coping with finials at each end of both ridges.

IMMACULATE CONCEPTION [ROMAN] CATHOLIC CHURCH, 1869

Jefferson, Marion County

There is some confusion about the date of construction of the Immaculate Conception Catholic Church. Some senior residents of Jefferson date it to 1840, while some publications date it to 1867. Records indicate that in April 1866 James M. Murphy and Allen Urquhart donated land for a Catholic church and school. The records also indicate "The contract for building the church was given by Rev. J. M. Giraud, a Catholic priest, to Mr. Benard Whitkorn of Nacogdoches, Texas. He was assisted by George Whitkorn and Tony Hillenkamp and the building was completed in 1869. "In 1870 William H. Ward deeded lots 10-11-12, block 28 on LaFayette and Vale Streets, to Rev. J. M. Giraud and the church was moved to [its present] location. . . ." The church was restored in 1967, and a narthex added at the entrance using the original doors and lancet-arched transom from the front entrance. (See Nomination Form, Historic American Buildings Survey, Department of the Interior [TEX -14]).

The plan of the church is rectangular, the length nearly twice the width, with a choir balcony over the entrance end of the nave; a chancel and two vesting rooms are at the opposite end of the space. The nave has a central and two side aisles. A stair with a right angle turn leads to the balcony from the left back corner of the nave. The form is simple: a rectangular solid with gabled roof and three-stage bell tower.

Four lancet-arched windows are uniformly spaced on either side wall of the church with a single similar but smaller window centered on each side of the narthex. The front gable of the church is treated as a classic pediment articulated by a molded entablature that joins the cornice of the eaves.

The top of the staged bell tower is covered by a galvanized metal hexagonal cone spire surmounted with a cross formed of bent metal. The belfry is square with a louvered lancet-arch on each side.

The wood frame construction is supported on uniformly spaced brick piers and covered by horizontal white clapboard siding. The building is pristine in its white wood surfaces with sunlight animating the walls and simple details in shade and shadow.

SAINT MARY'S [ROMAN] CATHOLIC CHURCH
AND SINAI HEBREW SYNAGOGUE, PRIOR TO 1869; 1876

Jefferson, Marion County

This complex of classically detailed buildings is an example of buildings whose functions have varied over the years, frequently referred to today as adaptive uses. The first structure, St. Mary's Catholic School, was built sometime before 1869, first serving as a residence owned by Mr. and Mrs. W. P. Williams. The property was purchased by Father John M.

Giraud on September 8, 1869, and immediately deeded to Father Burlando of Frederick County, Maryland, with the provision that it, in turn, be deeded to the Sisters of Charity of St. Vincent de Paul on their becoming organized in Texas. On November 16, 1871, the Sisters of Charity received the property; on May 20, 1874, however, financial difficulties forced a sale to the Sinai Hebrew Congregation of Beth-El. The synagogue assembly addition was constructed in 1876 by W. F. J. Graham. In 1954 the synagogue was secularized and sold to the Allen Wise Garden Club to be used as a playhouse and meeting facility.

These two frame structures with clapboard siding are joined by a covered passageway. The original school, identified by the Greek Revival tetrastyle portico, has the traditional two-story classic plan with central hall and similar rooms on both levels on either side of the corridor. Both structures are elevated above the sloping topography, the wood frame of the school resting on a brick foundation wall. The synagogue is partially supported by the remains of the foundation of a previous building plus brick piers with wood slatted infills between.

The synagogue is a single space, double height, nearly square, rectangular nave with balcony opposite the chancel and ark. The entrance is composed of a pair of centered curved-

The Synagogue

head four-panel double doors inset and hinged to elaborately paneled jambs opposite the chancel. An exterior covered stair leads to the balcony.

The school has a hipped roof over the enclosed portion of the building, with a similar roof form over the portico. The synagogue assembly building is covered by a gabled roof with a classic pediment at either end.

Though the two buildings were constructed at different times and for different functions, the Greek Revival details have been included in both; however, the classical influence is most obvious on the exterior of the school. This structure, which was built after the heyday of the Classic Revival period, exhibits many of the primary elements of the time, including the two-story portico with a surrounding entablature supported by four rectangular columns with capitols of the Tuscan order. Pilasters similar to the columns articulate the architectural detail at the juncture of the portico of the enclosed building. The front entrance double doors are surrounded by four-light side windows on either side and a five-light transom above. The six-over-six light double-hung windows are symmetrically fenestrated around the center line of the front door.

The synagogue assembly building, although carefully designed to harmonize with the school, is more austere. An

obvious difference is the strong vertical accent of the two-story, double-hung, wood sash, six-over-six light windows with round heads. Another variation from the original building, though still a prominent form of the classic period design, is the pedimented gabled roof delineated by the wood crown and bed moldings of the heavy cornice, which returns to accent the pediment at either end of the structure.

The School

House of the Seasons

Jefferson, Marion County

The House of the Seasons is a reflection of the affluence of Jefferson. Colonel Benjamin H. Epperson, an attorney, political leader, railroad developer, entrepreneur and friend of Sam Houston, built the home in 1872.

The plan of the house was originally a slightly off-square rectangle with a projecting two-story bay window extending from the left side. The original unattached kitchen was later joined to the house, making an "L" shaped plan. The wide central hall with a stair to the side and similar rooms on either side reflects classical design. A circular well in the hall of the second floor gives direct visual access from the first floor to the four-sided cupola crowning the roof. Each side of the cupola is glazed with different colored glass to represent the four seasons of the year: green for spring, yellow for summer, red for autumn and blue for winter.

The wood-frame dwelling was built during the Victorian period but it is a composite of the three architectural styles. Classical details include the Corinthian capitals and the fluted columns supporting the porch. The tall round-head windows of the second floor, the cupola and the curved head above the front entrance suggest Italian influence. The one-story veranda with baluster and newel posts above, the balustraded captain's walk, the square cupola with the curved pagoda-like roof surfaces, the metal parapet partially concealing the hipped roof and the molded fascia all contribute to the Victorian image.

R.S. TERRY HOME

Jefferson, Marion County

The R.S. Terry House was built in 1880 by a wealthy cotton producer at the height of the Victorian period when design was sometimes extravagant and on occasion even ostentatious. In addition, during Reconstruction architectural tastefulness was not a paramount concern for those with new wealth.

The Terry house, though modest in gingerbread adornments, exhibits a number of graceful hallmarks. Unlike so many of the asymmetrical plans and masses of the Victorian period, the simple layout with the central hall and similar rooms on either side offers symmetry similar to that of Greek Revival houses. The rectangular cube with the intersecting, steeply pitched gabled roof, unlike many of the more complex forms and the massing of this period, offers a harmonious composition.

The elaboration of detail unique to the Victorian period and found in the front porch was not unusual. While most of the columns of Victorian porches were slender and lathe turned with a variety of spindles and fusiform pieces, those of the Terry House are square with gingerbread brackets filling the juncture between the column top and the overhead beam.

The front façade, including the porch, is symmetrical, with six evenly spaced columns centered on the front door and the porch stair laced together by a banister rail and infilled with ornate palings. The identical lattice pattern of railing, palings and newel posts above each column, reflects the same order at the edge of the porch roof.

The symmetry of the tall Victorian windows, equally spaced on either side of the double front door and the similar fenestration at the second floor, offers a rhythmical order not often found during this architectural period. The front door head with the flat wood arched eyebrow overhead incorporates a glass transom above to admit light into the large central hall. Over the first floor window heads is a projecting nonsupporting lintel with a small triangular pediment in the center. The second-floor window heads are covered with a flat pediment. All windows are four-over-four. The apex of the gables is embellished with spindles, dentils, and other gingerbread ornament. Each gable also has a vent to allow air movement through the attic, allowing summer heat to escape.

THE METHODIST CHURCH, CIRCA 1880S

Jefferson, Marion County

The congregation of the First Methodist Church, the first organized in Marion County, was formed in 1844. Title to the property was granted in 1848. An original brick structure was constructed on the site of the present church some time during the 1850s. It was later condemned and razed, and the present church was erected on part of the surviving foundation. The present building, erected during the late 1880s, is the third church to stand near the top of a prominent slope.

It is a simple and elegant wood-frame, rectangular-plan building, with a bell tower extending above the gabled roof and entrance portico. The six tall stained-glass lancet windows are uniformly spaced on each side wall with two similar windows on either side of the entrance. The spire above the bell tower gives a strong vertical appearance; however, it appears somewhat slender when compared to the proportions of the belfry. The bell tower contains the famous original bell cast in 1858 by the Meneley Bell Foundry of Troy, New York. It is said that F. A. Schluter, in order to assure a "silvery tone," gave 1500 Mexican silver dollars to be melted down and included in the casting of the bell.

The double wood outlookers at the eaves support the overhang, and the white wood siding articulates the window openings, offering light, shade and shadow contrast between the various wall surfaces.

FRENCH'S TRADING POST

Beaumont, Jefferson County

John Jay French, through his international and local entrepreneurship, was an influential citizen during the latter days of the Republic and the early days of statehood. French's Trading Post, built in 1848, dealt both in goods from Texas and in those from out of state.

This residence was both a place of commerce and the home of the French family. The simplicity of the design and construction reflect the lifestyle, place and period. There are few embellishing details on the edifice. Although this house was constructed after Augustus Phelps introduced the Greek Revival style to Texas, the simplicity of the pioneer settlement period is still obvious.

The original house is a two-story rectangular cube with a saltbox to the rear. A wraparound one-story kitchen area attached to the house and the front porch were likely later additions.

Design details on this building include flat trim around the windows and front door, the transom light above the double door, the two opposing sidelights, the six-over-six window panes, the symmetry of the window placement and the porch banister and palings. There appears to be no planed or shaped molding.

"THE WOODLANDS"

Huntsville, Walker County

"The Woodlands," often referred to as "The Wigwam" (circa 1848), was the residence of the Sam Houston family for approximately ten years. The appearance of the original house is not known with certainty, but the restoration is probably as correct as possible based on the sketchy records that are available. The photographs of the house illustrate those portions that seem to be accurate for the period of the Houston tenure.

The date of the first phase of construction is unknown. The house evolved as did many of the early structures of the region with additions made when space was needed and financial

resources were available. The original was a one-room log cabin; a log crib was built opposite and the two were later connected by an open "dog run." The dog run was later enclosed to become the central hall with loft rooms above. Finally a back porch with small rooms at either end was added. The completed residence has six rooms. The house is symmetrical around the central hall. The original logs have been cased with wood siding.

The central hall, which extends from the front to the back, is a full room wide with double doors to the outside. Above the front door is a continuous vertical open grill to provide ventilation for the upper floor.

This structure was built during the period when Greek Revival style was popular in Texas, but "The Woodlands" exhibits no such details. It probably did not when the Houston family occupied it.

The elevation photograph is of the back façade, showing the symmetrical fenestration of the two back rooms, the windows and the porch with columns uniformly spaced on either side of the door. The primary portion of the house, covered by the gabled roof, is separate from the roof covering the porch and the two back rooms, and each has a different rake. The entire house sits on piers, thereby providing a physical as well as a visual separation of the first floor from the earth. Access to the half-story above is by two exterior stairs, one at the back porch, the other by the front porch.

"THE STEAMBOAT HOUSE"

Huntsville, Walker County

The "Steamboat House" was built in 1858 by Dr. Rufus Bailey as a gift to his daughter and son-in-law. Though built during the Greek Revival era, it has no rapport with the traditions or details of the period. Instead, the house was designed to imitate the image of the riverboats of the time.

This structure was leased to and was the last residence of Sam Houston and family after his retirement from public life. Moved from its original site in 1936, it is presently located in the Sam Houston Park in Huntsville.

At the time that the photograph was taken, the front stair had been removed because deterioration had made it unsafe. Other than this temporary modification (now restored), it is authentic to the period in which it was constructed.

Architecturally, this dwelling is unusual. Access to the major rooms is only from the outside along the galleries; the front and back rooms may be entered from the porches, a concept derived from the riverboat. The advantage of this is that each room is provided with cross ventilation; additionally, the porch roofs give shade to the exterior walls. Moreover, such an arrangement gives each room individual privacy.

The "steamboat" image is created by the twin towers at the front, suggesting a ship's bridge, together with the image of the riverboat smoke stacks. Colonnaded side porches with railings on the second level suggest a promenade.

The forms are simple; however, when joined as the "steamboat" configuration, the result is complex massing. The plan is unique: it is composed of single rooms at both of the two levels. The house is not unattractive.

JARDINE BROWNE HOUSE, 1849
Walker County

According to the Texas Historical Survey Committee (1968), Robert and Jane Jardine Browne built the east cabin of hewn pine logs set on walnut posts in 1849. The site was part of James Jardine (or Jordan) league, an 1835 land grant. The west cabin of sawn pine logs was added for a growing family. James F. Browne, a son born and reared here, added the lean-to bedroom, dining room and detached kitchen. The house was bought in 1940 from Browne heirs and restored in 1966 by Ben H. Powell, Jr.

The simplistic form of the original building and the additions is typical of early Texas architecture. The details are sophisticated for this period of limited tools and materials. The generous overhang of the roof, particularly over the front porch, protects the exterior walls from sun and water.

In addition to these practical considerations, the shade and shadow of the roof extension offer an aesthetic semblance of light and dark, articulating the solids and the voids of the mass while accenting the horizontal logs and the joints between each.

The overlap splice of the hewn sill log supporting the porch displays the craftsmanship and the ingenuity of the structural joinery. These two logs are probably not pinned together but simply shaped and fitted, allowing the cantilever extending from the supporting posts to mesh into a joint.

This log structure is a typical dog run house from the pioneer settlement period. The right crib, built in 1849, has notched and fitted hand-hewn logs with the traditional half-dovetail joints. The dog run was easily expanded by simply adding another crib and leaving the open breezeway between. A ladder within the dog run leads to a loft that was used for storage or for the traditional quarters of the older boys.

The later log addition incorporates sawn logs rather than hewn timbers. The corners in this construction are closely fitted with square notch assembly. In this house, the notch is protected from water penetration by the generous roof overhangs, eliminating rot potential.

The "mud cat" chimneys at the opposite ends of the log portion of the house are authentic reproductions of the originals. The back of the house, not shown in the illustrations, is another expansion of the first structure. It is covered with weather boarding and creates an "L-shaped" plan.

MONROE-COLEMAN HOUSE

Crockett, Houston County

This Greek Revival house was designed and constructed in 1854 with considerable sophistication yet simplicity of form and mass. The Greek temple form with pedimented portico joining the two elements creates a simple mass. The double front door surrounded by an overhead transom light, two side-lights, the four windows on the front of the house and the four dormers is symmetrically located and emphasizes the center axis of the façade. The four concentrically located chimneys add an additional order to the building.

The square columns with small capitals are a modification of the traditional Doric motif while the fascia and pediment moldings are typical of the Greek period.

Many Greek Revival houses of this period were likely framed by out-of-work shipwrights. Iron and steel ship hulls were introduced during the 1850s, causing many shipwrights to be displaced and to seek employment as house carpenters. The framing of the Monroe-Coleman House is assembled with join-ture traditionally used in wood ships. Mortise and tenon joints

were used in the post and beam and stud framing. Diagonal bracing was also cut and fitted with similar joints. This construction provided excellent framing and jointing, structurally solid under all load conditions.

An interesting detail of the chimney design is the separation of the upper flue masonry from the wood siding of the house. The clapboard is scribed to the masonry as high as the corbeled brick levels; however, the upper chimney separation from the wall simplifies the cutting and fitting of the siding and fascia as well as minimizing the possibility of water accumulating between the materials.

During the restoration of this house, Raiford Stripling found that several of the interior walls were filled with dry stacked brick, causing the sill beams to sag between supports. He speculated that these brick infills may have been placed inside the interior walls to discourage rats.

TWO

CENTRAL TEXAS, POST OAK SAVANNAH AND BLACKLAND PRAIRIE

Before independence, Central Texas was settled by Anglo-Americans, primarily from the southern United States, and some African Americans brought as slaves. After independence, Germans, French (Alsatian), Czechs, Poles and Irish arrived. Most settlers wanted land, but some were escaping religious and political oppression in their home countries. Eking out an existence on the frontier while trying to survive the raids of hostile Indians, sickness and extreme weather conditions made life difficult. In spite of such adversities, many of the new immigrants prospered.

Central Texas includes the Blackland Prairie and the Post Oak Savannah—moderately flat country. Two rivers, the Colorado and the Brazos, have built large fertile flood plains of dark clay or reddish-brown calcareous clay loams, which are valuable as tillable agricultural land. The rest of the region is composed of dark-colored calcareous clays, some clay loams and some acid sandy loams. Much of this land is appropriate for crops such as cotton; large portions are nonproductive, however, and have traditionally been used for grazing.

The climate in the Post Oak Savannah and the Blackland Prairie is not significantly different from that of East Texas and the timberland region. Thirty-two to 44 inches of annual precipitation—somewhat less than the yearly Gulf Coast average—is expected.

Forest vegetation consists primarily of post oak, live oak, black jack oak and some hickory and pecan along streams. Most of these woods are not good building materials and early settlers were compelled to use twisted oaks for their modest log buildings. Later as sawn timber became available, builders turned to traditional frame construction, creating some outstanding homes.

Log Construction

The log cabin, sometimes called a "pole shack," was one of the earliest Anglo-American forms and the most rudimentary. Equipped only with a bare earth floor and a stick-and-dirt chimney, a pole shack was usually built for temporary occupancy in the first difficult years when a pioneer family was becoming established on the land.

Building a log house was work intensive, requiring heavy labor to harvest timber and to move it to the building site (with the assistance of draft animals) and many additional man-hours to shape the individual logs for assembly. Lumber for the traditional log cabin was always hewn or hand-split. Logs were cut to a precise length, then shaped on the horizontal surfaces with an adz to allow water to run off on the outside of the wall and to give a smoother surface on the interior. The end of each timber was carefully notched with saw and ax for a precise fit. The logs were then stacked into position, a simple, rapid process. Once the materials had been prepared, most single-crib log structures were assembled in a day.

"V" Notch

Three basic techniques for joining hewn logs were used: the "V" notch, the half-dovetail notch and the square notch. The traditional "V" notch was probably the most popular, perhaps because it shed water by gravity and was easily assembled. Before tailoring the joints, each log was hewn on the two opposite sides and cut to the right length. The "V" was cut by making two shallow saw cuts on opposite sides approximately four to six inches from the end. The cut was at a slight angle perpendicular to the hewn faces of the log and to the longitudinal axis. The wood between the cuts and at the end of the log was split apart and removed, leaving a convex "V" notch. The log to be placed on top was traditionally cut with an ax or hatchet in the shape of a concave "V," or notch to fit inside the convex "V." When assembled, the log with the concave "V" was placed at right angles to the receiving log with the convex notch, thereby locking the two pieces together at the joint. As additional logs with these cuts were laid, the weight compressed the joints, securing and interlocking the four corners of the structure.

Because of the upturned notch, water would drain from the assembly, maintaining a dry joint and preventing rot. Log structures a hundred or more years old of tight grain wood—heart pine, white oak, cedar, cypress—with this joint are still in fine condition today.

The half-dovetail assembly provided an interlocking system which assured that each log would retain its position in the jointed construction without shifting. In addition, the interlocking nature of this joint and the sloping cuts of each notch allowed water to drain by gravity, minimizing the possibility of standing water. These logs were numbered with Roman numerals to identify the position of each timber. In addition, each log was marked with a chiseled symbol to identify the exact corner of the building, the direction of the notch and which side of the log was to face up and which side out.

Half dovetail

The square notch, sometimes called the "quarter" notch provided a bearing surface for each log but did not lock the logs together. In order to secure each timber in place, a spike or dowel was sometimes toenailed through two logs at the joint overlap. The notch was prominent in Texas and may have been derived from the half dovetail as an easier cut requiring less sophisticated craftsmanship. Another distinct disadvantage to the square notch is that water will not drain from the flat surfaces. The wood therefore is more likely to decompose over time.

Doors and windows were cut into the log structure after assembly. The openings were framed with sawn and hand-planed lumber. To make sawn timber, a tree was felled with an ax or cross-cut saw, then ripped into timber for boards, beams and framing with a vertical pit saw. This simple device was operated by two men, one above on a scaffold pulling the saw up and one below pulling the saw down, thus making a vertical cut as a rip saw.

Roofs were usually gabled with enough pitch to shed rainwater, ice and snow easily. Roof overhangs were usually provided on all four sides of the house. Extending the top two longitudinal rafters two to three feet created the roof overhang. The rafters, usually cantilevered beyond the plate of the two supporting walls, offered a frame to secure the roof deck and allow rainwater to drain beyond the outside walls.

Frequently a porch was added and might include a "Louisiana" roof, part of the roof framing system with the same slope over the porch as the main part of the building or an applied porch usually attached to the front or rear wall of the house and to (or below) the lower eave of the primary roof. The loft or garret directly below the roof provided sleeping accommodations for children.

The "ridgepole-and-purlin" roof was one of the most primitive and least common. The logs in the end walls were cut and notched to accommodate the purlins. This created forty-five-degree triangular shaped gables with purlins set back to line up with the angled form.

The "Anglo western" roof with ridgepole has a very low pitch with the unshaped ridgepole supported directly on the two top logs of the end walls, the rafters resting on the ridgepole and the two longitudinal wall plates.

Square Notch

Roofs were also constructed of smaller timbers that served as rafters. These were nailed or pegged to the two top longitudinal logs and at the top of the gable, sometimes incorporating a ridgepole. In most of the earlier log buildings, the roof rafters were not shaped and often made of cedar left in the round with the bark still attached. As sawn timber became more easily accessible, these rafters were shaped for sawn-roof decking spaced horizontally four to six inches apart and nailed to the upper face of the rafter frame.

The most primitive roofing was clapboard shaped with a froe, split approximately six to eight inches wide and sawed to length from white oak, post oak, burr oak or pine. Clapboards were placed over purlins with the grain running ridge to eaves, overlapped at all joints, held in place by "weight poles," and fastened perpendicular to the clapboards, running parallel to the ridge and eaves. If nails or pins were available, the clapboards were simply nailed to the purlins, making a cleaner surface and eliminating the weight poles.

Hand-split cedar or oak shakes and split and tapered shingles were introduced during the nineteenth century. The shakes or shingles were fastened to the decking in an overlapping pattern so that gravity carried rainwater down the roof slope, preventing penetration through the joints.

Chinking was the last step in constructing a log building. The gaps between logs were usually filled with mud, moss, grass or rocks. More sophisticated chinking techniques included cut-

ting small pieces of wood and driving them into the opening with a mallet. Walls were frequently plastered both inside and outside with mud to which grass or moss had been added to improve bonding.

Chimneys and fireplaces took a number of forms. The most basic, usually confined to more primitive cabins and applied to the exterior, was the "mud cat" or "stick-and-mud" chimney. They were made of mud clay and supported by a wood-crib surround composed of small logs three to six inches in diameter. Because the mud eventually weakened or eroded as it absorbed moisture, the mud-cat chimney was not permanent. In addition, the wood of the crib frequently caught fire, endangering the main structure. As settlers learned from their experiences with mud-cat-chimney fires, they leaned the flue away from the log wall, countering the horizontal load with a wooden pole to support the flue. If the crib ignited, the resident simply knocked the diagonal pole away, allowing the blazing "cat" to fall from the house and preventing the spread of the fire.

Stone or brick fireplaces and chimneys were usually constructed by craftsmen skilled in making

lime mortar, cutting and laying stone and building fireboxes and chimney flues of the right size and shape to draw well and produce the most heat for warmth and cooking.

Historian Terry G. Jordan has recorded the late 1840s account of W.R. Strong of Cook County of a log cabin raising. "People were

Square Notch

mighty good to help each other in those days. . . . If you built a house, everybody for ten miles would come and help raise it. . . . My house was a log cabin fourteen feet square with a stick and dirt chimney covered with boards. . . . I put the logs up round when I built my house in the spring, then in the fall I took a chopping ax and hewed the logs down smooth, then I cut chinking out of little poles mostly and chinked the cracks and plastered them over with mud. I hewed out puncheons for the floor. . . ." (See Jordan, *Texas Log Buildings: A Folk Architecture* [Austin: University of Texas Press, 1978], pp. 105-07.)

The log cabin was replaced by the log house—a second-generation dwelling—which was larger than a cabin and built of carefully hewn and neatly notched timbers that were then tightly chinked. The dwelling generally had plank floors and a gracefully shaped chimney of stone or brick. Unlike the cabin, the log house was normally constructed by professional or semi-professional carpenters, itinerant craftsmen who went from place to place building houses for hire.

The concept of the log house originated in Sweden, was borrowed by the Danes and Germans and imported to America by the Swedes at their settlement in the Delaware Water Gap, Pennsylvania. The Germans introduced their concept of log-house construction through the Lehigh Valley in Pennsylvania and later in Central Texas. There is evidence that the Scots learned log construction from the Scandinavians and also brought their techniques to America.

The pioneers who constructed these buildings were highly skilled craftsmen, working only with handmade tools and limited technology to build structures of superb workmanship. Skills included cutting, sawing, planing, jointing, joining, chiseling and fitting wood; working with brick, stone and adobe; cutting, forging, welding, bending, shaping and riveting metal. Each piece of material, structural member and ornamental feature represented a builder's handiwork and, often, his ingenuity as new techniques evolved alongside the traditional construction methods.

The most distinctive configuration was the "dog-run" or "dog trot" house. Thought to have originated in Georgia, it consisted of two cribs separated by an open but covered central breezeway. Many dog-run log houses evolved from a single log structure; as the family expanded, a second crib was added. The name dog run is derived from the fact that family dogs found the shade and the breeze during the summer as comfortable as did the residents. Frequently the dog run was enclosed during the winter, adding a third room. Many still survive and have been preserved or restored as historic structures.

Many houses of this period also had a loft and, in some cases a full second story, including a dog run at the upper level with an exterior stair to the second floor. As the idea of through ventilation was developed and accepted in later houses, it became popular with the builders and owners. A wide central hall served as a receiving room, as well as connecting the other major rooms.

Early settlers faced buildings to the south to minimize the hot summer sun (high in the sky during the middle of the day), and to maximize exposure to the winter sun, which is low and warms the windows, porches and exterior walls. A well-crafted log structure provides for most of the human comforts of a house. Carefully crafted logs provided excellent insulation against the heat and the cold. It was easy to heat a log structure with an open fireplace or, later, with an iron stove. In addition, the log structure was an excellent deterrent to hostile attack.

In the 1840s, as water and steam power became available, timbers were sawn by a high-speed, rotating circular blade, speeding up the process and substantially reducing labor. These innovations were introduced primarily by southern Anglo settlers. Sawn timber gradually began to be used for siding, which, when applied over the log building, not only minimized air infiltration, water penetration, wood rot and heat loss or gain but also improved appearance. In the mid-1800s, complete wood-frame and clapboard construction was introduced. The powered sawmill also ushered in the board-and-batten construction technique, whereby the joints of vertical boards—load-bearing walls—were covered by a thin strip of wood (or batten), reducing or eliminating air and water penetration.

BROWN-WOODLIEF LOG HOUSE, PRIOR TO 1828
Present Site Near Washington-on-the Brazos, Washington County

The Brown-Woodlief house, a fine example of pioneer architecture, is a hand-hewn, dog-run cabin. It was originally located on the Hidalgo Bluffs overlooking the Brazos River approximately four-and-a-half miles northeast of Washington-on-the-Brazos. Eventually the dwelling became the property of Mrs. Elliott Goodwin. Goodwin's heirs—who had a keen interest in preserving the structure—gave the house to the present owners, Mr. and Mrs. Thomas A. Bullock, with the proviso that it be restored as an accurate example of early Texas construction. The heirs also stipulated that owners secure a Texas historic site marker to provide for its authenticity. The house—named for prominent Texian settler and

soldier J. Deveraux Woodlief—is now located on the Bullock farm near Washington-on-the-Brazos.

The simple form, two square log cribs tied together by a single roof, exhibits the basic concepts of climate control. Two porches and the covering roofs provide shade from the hot summer sun but allow the afternoon sun of winter to warm the interior. The logs of the two opposing rooms are cut from oak, cedar, red gum and cottonwood and are notched at the corners with square-cut joints. Two native stone fireplaces and chimneys are laid up with the flat side of the stones positioned horizontally, typical of the period masonry.

DR. ASA HOXEY HOUSE, 1833

Independence, Washington County

The Hoxey house (1833) was built by one of the first Anglo-American settlers in the Independence area, Dr. Asa Hoxey, a man of ability and considerable estate for the day. He held land, slaves and livestock, and was a successful farmer.

The dwelling is located at the crest of a gently sloping hill, frequently called the Brazos Bluffs, and faces north overlooking the Brazos River and flood plain. This site provides good drainage, continuous breezes, an excellent view and command of the plains below. Though in disuse, the house has weathered reasonably well and has maintained much of its original character. While still structurally sound, it should be restored to its original condition.

The house appears to have been built in three different sections. The small middle kitchen may have been the first structure, the large house with the back porch facing the 1936 Centennial Monument came second and the end opposite the kitchen was last. The kitchen floor is approximately two feet below the floor of the two adjoining parts and has a large stone fireplace in the common west wall. A stone chimney—apparently added later—has been replaced with a metal stack. The porch columns on the first level and the windows on the upper level are not uniformly spaced. It is likely that function prevailed over form in the design of the openings.

Most of the wood framing materials are hand cut, including the exterior siding; interior walls are hand cut and planed from cedar stock. At one time, this house was considered attractive, well detailed and comfortable.

FANTHORP INN, 1834

Anderson, Grimes County

The Fanthorp Inn is one of the earliest Anglo-American buildings in Central Texas. It has been purchased by the Texas Parks and Wildlife Department and fully restored to its 1830s condition. Henry Fanthorp of England was the original builder, owner and operator of the inn. Two stagecoach lines met in front of the house, and the residence became a stage stop known as the Fanthorp Inn. Many early Texas settlers and leaders of the Republic were overnight guests at the hostelry during their travels through the region. In 1845, the citizens of the town, then called Fanthorp, renamed the village in honor of Kenneth L. Anderson, the last vice-president of the Republic of Texas, who died at the inn while traveling.

The form of the original building was simple; however, the many modifications and additions over the years developed an L-plan, causing more complex massing.

The double front porch—an outside space created by the roof overhang and the evenly spaced columns—offers the most visual appeal. The horizontal emphasis of the second floor, the railing and palings emphasize the space. This composition gives a simple visual rhythm and order to the façade. The other surfaces are without decoration or detail other than the uniformly spaced windows on the upper and lower floors. Each of the upstairs windows have a six-over-six pane pattern, and the lower floor windows have a nine-over-six pattern.

The material of the structure is primarily cedar. The front of the building, which was likely constructed first, is made of cedar logs that carry halfway up into the second floor. It appears that at some time the owner added a half story stud wall (or knee wall) above the cedar logs to provide for a second floor. Other parts of the house are built of large wood framing that is supported on stone pier foundations with mortise and tenon joints tying the structure together.

The Fanthorp Inn is a historic site open to the public.

The inn before restoration

WINEDALE STAGECOACH INN, THE LEWIS WAGNER FARMSTEAD, 1834, 1848

Winedale, Washington County

The Winedale Stagecoach Inn was built in 1834 by William S. Townsend using locally available cedar. The original building was one large room with a fireplace and a loft for sleeping quarters. It was purchased by Samuel K.Lewis in 1848 and enlarged to its present plan featuring a symmetrical two-level dog run through the center. For many years the house was known as the Samuel Lewis Stopping Place.

The generous two-level veranda, with an exterior stair at the extreme end of the porch (probably designed to conserve interior space), is symmetrically designed to cover the entire façade of the house. The veranda shades the front wall from the summer sun, protects the windows and doors from the elements and allows a comfortable outdoor space for residents to enjoy the pleasant breezes. A second open stair within the dog run offers architectural and functional variety.

HUTCHINSON-KORTH HOMESTEAD, CIRCA 1836

Near Washington-on-the-Brazos, Washington County

Deed records indicate that this structure was built on a land grant from the Mexican government to Samuel Gates in 1824. In 1842 the property was bought by "Captain" Burrel B. Hutchinson, a prosperous farmer and holder of forty-six slaves. The descedents of Burrell Hutchinson sold the property to William and Minnie Korth in 1888. The Korth family then sold the property to Mr. and Mrs. Tom Bullock of Houston in 1969. Tom Bullock, an architect, has restored the home to its 1890 appearance, attempting to "keep the old impurity," even while making practical changes. Restored elements include doors, stained glass, transom and other pieces of the house found stored in the farmstead buildings.

The form of the house is simple: a gabled roof, a front porch, front doors at both levels and symmetrical window fenestration on either side of the porch on both floors. The front two rooms of the Hutchinson-Korth Homestead date to 1836 when the house was built. The dog run was constructed of hand-hewn cedar with oak posts and assembled with round wood pegs. The upstairs window panes are twelve-over-eight lights and much earlier than the two-over-two lights of the first floor. Both upper- and lower-level doors are single, but the lower door has flanking sidelights and a transom light above. The porch is adorned by four evenly spaced, slender columns at both levels with small capitols and bases applied to each.

The most unusual embellishment is the porch railing on both levels. These railings were probably purchased through a woodworking plant outside of Texas that produced Victorian icons and shipped them to the site by river and by overland carriers.

CAVITT HOUSE, 1838-1848

Wheelock, Robertson County

Among the first residents of this house were W. D. Moore and the widow Ann Cavitt, her seven sons and nineteen slaves. The Cavitt family resided at Dunn's Fort in Robertson County, while slaves built a modest log cabin on Ann's land in Wheelock in 1836. The Cavitts lived in the cabin, located a few miles off the Camino Real, known to Anglo settlers as the "Old Spanish Trail" or the "San Antonio Trail"; that cabin now stands in the yard of the Armstrong Inn. Mrs. Cavitt married her deceased husband's nephew, Cavitt Armstrong, and, with the assistance of a gifted carpenter, they built the inn between 1838 and 1848. It was one of the largest and most attractive overnight stops for the stagecoach transporting travelers between Nacogdoches and San Antonio. Many early Texans, including Sam Houston and other famed individuals, dined and slept here.

The building is large for an early residence but remains simple in form and mass while showing care and sophistication in design and construction. The temple form and square box columned double veranda, are not adorned with traditional details but show considerable Greek Revival influence. The six columns are evenly spaced and symmetrically located, while the second floor banister rail and palings suggest a clear order and strong design. The double front doors on both levels are centered and surrounded by transom and side lights. The windows on both levels are positioned symmetrically around the front doors.

The plan has a traditional central hall with two similar rooms on either side, six fireplaces, and four porches. The hall continues through the house to provide living space and ventilation. The house is constructed of heart pine, cedar and cypress siding and wood trim that has been hand planed and shaped.

HUNT-HARDY HOUSE, CIRCA 1840

Gay Hill, Washington County

The Hunt-Hardy house is a strong example of the design and construction of a Greek Revival house with the traditional appointments of the period. The Greek temple form is evident but significantly modified by the addition of the salt box to the back of the house. The six symmetrically placed round columns are small in diameter and have small Doric capitals at the top.

There doesn't appear to be any entasis in the columns, however; each column has a base, which is not consistent with the Greek Doric order and is probably not original.

That the house may have been modified at some point is suggested by the different angles at the end elevations of the horizontal molding lines of the entablature. There is no

HUNT-HARDY HOUSE *continued*

pediment as the structure appears today, but it would likely have been included in the original Greek design. There are two double doors at the center of the front façade, traditional transom lights and side lights, and symmetrically placed windows flanking the doors on both levels. It is possible that, at a later date, an original portico may have been replaced by the long front porch with small columns supporting the roof.

All the window patterns are nine-over-nine, surrounded with flat trim. There is no indication of any molding other than the fascias which may be a later modification to the house.

MISS SALLY THOMPSON SCHOOL, CIRCA 1840

Anderson, Grimes County

This pleasant Greek Revival residence was originally used as a school and reported to have been owned and operated by Miss Sally Thompson. It is located near the edge of the village across from the Fanthorp Inn on the original road into Anderson.

The traditional temple form of the house is obvious with the square box columns and Doric type capitals supporting the pediment of the portico. The house is pleasantly scaled and proportioned. Small scale moldings follow the fascias of the pediment and the eaves of the roof. The front door identifies the axis of the symmetrical window placement. The window composition is a six-over-six pattern.

The siding is joined at each corner by a flat planed trim board that articulates the walls and accents the corners. The white siding provides a pleasant contrast to the shades and shadows of the various surfaces.

GENERAL JAMES W. BARNES PLANTATION HOUSE, 1842
"Prairie Woods," Grimes County

General James W. Barnes served as an officer in the Confederate Army after a successful career as a businessman and a planter. He first constructed this building in 1842 as a two-story house with one room on each floor. It was a log house with a fireplace. Later in 1858, he added a large central hall, a matching room to the left of the original log structure, with at least four smaller rooms behind that. Barnes refinished the entire exterior in the Greek Revival style.

The complete 1852 addition is constructed of traditional stud framing with wood weatherboard siding. The large center hall has outdoor entrances at either end to allow access and ventilation during the warm summers. The walls of the later construction are insulated with cotton seed and attached cotton fibers.

The unadorned mass is composed of a series of simple forms including the steeply pitched hip roof, a modified rectangular two-story plan and a portico to emphasize the front doors at both levels.

The front façade is composed of four-over-four sash windows on each side of a center portico with a balcony and entrances. The horizontal and vertical dimensions are well-proportioned. The double, four-paneled front doors create an inviting entrance and provide maximum air movement through the house. The side lights on both sides of the doors on the first and second floors provide for natural illumination within the large enclosed first-floor hall and the small second-floor corridor. The columns supporting the balcony, the roof and pediment are square and made of wood. There is a

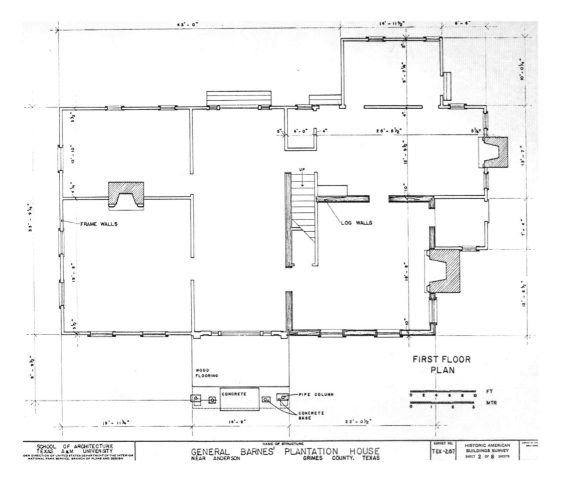

FRAME WALLS

LOG WALLS

UP

**FIRST FLOOR
PLAN**

WOOD
FLOORING

CONCRETE

PIPE COLUMN

CONCRETE
BASE

FT

MTR

SCHOOL OF ARCHITECTURE
TEXAS A&M UNIVERSITY
(DER DIRECTION OF UNITED STATES DEPARTMENT OF THE INTERIOR
NATIONAL PARK SERVICE, BRANCH OF PLANS AND DESIGN

NAME OF STRUCTURE
GENERAL BARNES' PLANTATION HOUSE
NEAR ANDERSON   GRIMES COUNTY, TEXAS

SURVEY NO.
TEX-287

HISTORIC AMERICAN
BUILDINGS SURVEY
SHEET 2 OF 8 SHEETS

modest square wood Doric capital at the top and a wood plinth at the base. The baluster at the balcony encloses the three open sides.

The fascia at the roof's edge is adorned with a tier of wood dentils with two additional rows attached to the top of the walls directly below the soffit. This triple row of inset dentils continues on the two oblique fascias of the pediment.

At this time, the house is in a rather poor state of repair, but the current owner is in the process of restoring it to its original condition.

DRAWINGS ARE SHOWN IN RESTORED CONDITION   NOTE: DIMENSIONS INDICATE PRESENT CONDITION

SOUTH (FRONT) ELEVATION

BAPTIST CHURCH, 1844, 1855
Anderson, Grimes County

The present Anderson Baptist Church was erected in 1855 after the original 1844 building had been destroyed by fire. It was built at the height of the Greek Revival movement and clearly derives from the temple form. The white pediment above the stone facade is an exemplary detail of the Greek style. The church is unadorned, simple in form, proportion, scale and fenestration.

Features include three symmetrically placed front portals, the middle considerably larger with double doors and a fifteen light transom. The two flanking doors likely at one time also had transom lights above; however, because of the addition of window air conditioners, these lights appear to be enclosed. The four tall windows on each of the side walls also appear to be modifications from an earlier period with unmatched masonry infill at the heads closing the dimensional changes. The bell tower and spire are later modifications having little scale or proportional relation to the building.

JOHN F. MARTIN HOUSE, 1845

Anderson, Grimes County

The John Martin house has a typical Greek temple form illustrated by the center two-story portion that exhibits a certain elegance. The one-story side rooms create a more complex massing to the total building and were probably added at a later date as suggested by the awkward roof junctures at the portico. The extension of the upper roof that forms the double porch creates a traditional temple pediment with wood molding architrave around the fascia line. It appears that at one time there were probably applied capitals at the top of the square box columns. The banister rail and palings at the second level offer order to the front of the building. The middle column at the first floor may have been added at a later time to provide

additional support to the second-floor porch; however, the odd spacing is unsympathetic to the proportioning of the traditional image of the Greek façade.

The asymmetrically located double doors on each level and the windows in the counter position of the front façade displace the congruence. All the windows are six-over-six patterns.

GENERAL JEROME B. ROBERTSON HOUSE, 1845-1849

Independence, Washington County

General Jerome Bonaparte Robertson came to Texas from Kentucky after raising a company of volunteers to serve in the Texas revolution and arrived after the Battle of San Jacinto. After Robertson put his affairs in order in Kentucky, he returned to Texas and served as a physician, mayor of Washington-on-the-Brazos and an Indian campaigner. In 1861, Robertson raised a company of Texans to serve in the Confederacy, moved through the ranks until appointed brigadier general and succeeded the command of General John Bell Hood. He was wounded three times during the conflict. In 1864, he returned to Texas to recruit troops for the Army of Northern Virginia and to command reserves.

This house is located on a high sandstone rock outcropping that receives good ventilation during the warm months, good ground and surface water nearby. It is one of the earliest Anglo-American sites in Central Texas. Independence is on the old La Bahia Trail, the east-west connection from the Gulf coast near Corpus Christi to the Camino Real. Considerable trade and contraband were probably moved along this route.

The dwelling is a one-story frame house with clapboard siding and gabled roof. The house has gone through several modifications during its history (several splices have been made in the siding which supports the speculation that changes have been made). The building may have had a porch completely across the front; however, at least one and possibly two rooms have been added under this roof. Most likely the original column locations have been moved to support the roof. The stone chimneys have been plastered over.

JOHN CAMPBELL LOG HOUSE, CIRCA 1850

Seguin, Guadalupe County

The John Campbell dog-run house is a fine model of the traditional two crib log structure of the pioneer settlement period. The house was originally built outside the city of Seguin and recently moved into a public park in an effort to preserve an example of local architectural heritage. The restoration is well done, and the unadorned form of the house is pure.

DR. BERKELEY PERRY CURRY HOUSE, 1850

Old Gay Hill, five miles west of Independence, Washington County

The image offered by the Dr. Berkeley Perry Curry residence in the 1850s was one of affluence. Obviously the family had a sense of aesthetic appreciation and enjoyed living in comfort. The house was built during the Greek Revival period and has been more recently modified with some ornamental detail of the Victorian era. The most prominent ornamentation is the front portico and pediment supported by four symmetrically located box columns with Doric capitals and wood molding at the corners. The front door is flanked on either side by side lights with a transom light above. The wood molding on the fascias is thin in scale and contributes to the detail. The portico is well proportioned and visually pleasing. The outlookers below the soffit of the pediment were likely added at a later time as structural reinforcement or possibly a Victorian adornment.

HUMPHREY-ERSKINE HOUSE, 1850

Seguin, Guadalupe County

The Humphrey-Erskine house has a rectangular plan and an uncomplicated form derived from the classic period of the time. It may be difficult to see this building as a Greek classic, but it does exhibit the simple temple form. The five square columns, with small Doric type capitals on each, support the galleried veranda second floor and the roof. The banister rail and palings incorporated with the columns offer visual order and rhythm to the façade. The exterior stair to the second level porch is a unique architectural feature that offers additional animation to this face. There are four doors with two located on each level and positioned one above the other. The windows are placed in a similar configuration and continue to give a visual elegance to the house.

The house is constructed of concrete, mortised frame and clapboard. Dr. Richard Parks, a chemist, developed concrete and introduced it to Seguin as a new technology widely used in residential construction during the 1850s. This material was used in forming the structural floors and walls of the Humphrey-Erskine house. Because of this new technology, the residence had many new additions in its early life. These additions required concrete studding that may have contributed to the differences in the column and window spacing.

JOSE NAVARRO HOUSE, OFFICE AND KITCHEN, CIRCA 1850

San Antonio, Bexar County

José Antonio Navarro played several significant roles in the settlement of Texas. He supported the concept of Texas independence, first from Spain and later from Mexico, served as mayor of San Antonio, as a legislator to the State of Coahuila and Texas, signed the Texas Declaration of Independence and contributed to the constitution of the Republic of Texas. Navarro was also a successful rancher and merchant.

The José Navarro home at South Larado and West Nueva streets is composed of his office, the house and a detached kitchen. The structures are of adobe, caliche block, plaster

JOSE NAVARRO HOUSE, OFFICE AND KITCHEN *continued*

and limestone. The architecture of the three buildings reflects the simplicity of the Spanish Colonial and Mexican styles of the 1850s.

The complex is designed as a series of simple forms arranged as a composition of solids and spaces. The siting of the buildings provides private outdoor spaces on three sides, the back and between the individual structures. The house faces the street and is set back from the front property line, while the office sits at the corner of the two intersecting streets, giving privacy to the interior yards.

The office, which also served at one time as a store, is a simple plastered caliche stone rubble cube with quoins at the corners, a hipped roof, a soffit overhang and a thin fascia at the roof edges. The quoining ties the abutting walls together at the corners interlocking the stone walls and giving structural stability. The first floor herring-bone pattern wooden double doors and the windows above are symmetrically located on the front façade (west face), each with transom lights overhead. The asymmetrical fenestration on the east and south elevations follow functional requirements and offer visual interest. The exterior stair to the second floor on the east wall gives access to the upper level as well as adding form, shade and shadow.

The house, located immediately next to the office is a simple form, different from the configuration of the office. The thick stone walls are covered with a pitched roof to the front and back and a porch roof with a more shallow rake. The four columns across the front support the porch roof and a balustrade across the front and to the sides of the the porch together offer visual harmony.

The detached kitchen is a smaller version of the house, with a front and back porch and a hipped roof. The thick adobe walls are plastered and painted white in sympathy with the two white neighboring structures.

"SEBASTOPOL," COLONEL JOSHUA YOUNG HOUSE, 1851

Seguin, Guadalupe County

The house known as "Sebastopol" was built by Colonel Joshua Young for his daughter, Mrs. Katherine LeGette, circa 1851. This house is of the simplest form and was designed and built as a one-story house with a basement at the back. It has several unique features including a reservoir in the roof that is concealed by the unadorned broad entablature. The square box columns, with a square capital on each, spaced on three sides of the structure, suggest a modified peristyle form. The house, built of concrete, has a near square foundation plan with a veranda surrounding part of three sides of a "T" plan at the main floor

Although the columns are not uniformly spaced, they are in concert with the banister rail and palings. The double front door with transom and side lights is typical of the period. A small pediment is placed at the door head with molding and plinth at the jambs. The windows at the front of the house are symmetrically located on either side of the front door.

EDWARD HENKEL HOUSE, 1851
Round Top, Fayette County

This home, now a museum, has a simple plan that is two rooms deep, one room wide and two stories high. The generous front porch shelters the windows, doors and front wall of the major rooms on the first floor.

Outside stairs rise from the front porch and lead to a landing at the garret or loft level. The roof has a generous overhang, that simultaneously shelters the exterior stair and the east wall. Two longitudinal joists are exposed and integrated as part of the roof system, giving support to the rafters while offering protection from possible deflection of the cantilevered roof overhang. In addition, a two-level wood column supports the corner of the roof overhang at the northeast corner and completes the framing support.

STAGE COACH TAVERN, 1851

Chappell Hill, Washington County

Austin became the capitol of State of Texas in 1846. Many travelers went by stage between Austin, Houston and Waco as the state developed. The inn at Chappell Hill became an important overnight stopping point because of the comfortable accommodations, good food and its pleasant Greek Revival architecture.

Robert Wooding Chappell settled in Washington County in 1838 and purchased 1,280 acres of land. Mary Hargrove

STAGE COACH TAVERN *continued*

Haller, his granddaughter, purchased 100 acres of land from her sister and divided the site into three-acre lots with streets and alleys. She named the community "Chappell Hill," in honor of her grandfather.

In 1850 and 1851 Mary and her husband Jacob began constructing their home and inn. The Greek Revival building has fourteen rooms and a large rectangular dining area at the back that deviates from the traditional symmetrical plan but was built to entertain several guests. The first floor plan consists of a central entrance and hall with a parlor, bedroom and dining room on either side. All of the guest bedrooms are located upstairs.

Many well-built, well-preserved stage inns are restored and have survived the passage of time, while some still lack attention. The Chappell Hill tavern was bought and restored by Mr. and Mrs. Harvin Moore in 1976 as their residence. The late Harvin Moore, was a noted restoration architect from Houston.

The house is an uncomplicated rectangular form, symmetrical in plan and elevation. The windows and front doors are symmetrical on each façade in vertical accord. Both doors have side lights incorporated into their composition and the door on the first floor is topped with a transom light.

The portico exhibits tapered square box columns, Doric type capitals and pilasters supporting the architrave and roof of the porch. In addition to the windows and doors, the balcony rail and palings offer a distinct order to the façade.

The cornice frieze that encircles the entire house is an excellent example of ornamental Greek icon or image. The leader heads for the down spouts are embellished with the Texas star and were probably adopted by metal fabricators from Augustus Phelp's metal leaves.

Stone and cedar were gathered locally and sawn near the site for building materials. Tin, nails, paint and plaster were not locally available and had to be hauled overland from Houston.

WILBARGER HOUSE, 1852

Bastrop, Bastrop County

This Greek Revival two-story, heart-pine frame clapboard house, has a gabled roof and was originally a simple temple form with a two-story portico and a one-story extension to the rear. The dwelling has a central hall with similar rooms on either side. Later additions and alterations have created a more complex massing. The windows are symmetrically positioned on both levels around the central front door. The side walls are fenestrated by equally spaced windows at each level. The windows are identical, with a six-over-six-pane composition; all retain the original shutters.

The portico is supported by eight square box columns with Doric type capitals, four on each level. A banister and palings on three sides of the second floor balcony are articulated between the columns to provide an order and rhythm for the portico.

A plain pilaster covers each corner of the building with a Doric type capital at the top of each. The fascia molding is cut from a pattern of the Greek Revival period, which wraps around the corners at the end walls.

The original stone chimneys were later replaced with brick.

CONRAD SCHUEDDEMAGEN HOUSE, 1852

Round Top, Fayette County

The Conrad Schueddemagen House is a replica of the Saxony home of Carl Siegismunde Bauer, built by Schueddemagen for Bauer's daughter and her husband. The steep gabled roof is an adaptation of European architectural influence brought to Texas by the German immigrants to force snow to slide from the steep rake. Although there is little snow accumulation in Texas, the high gable allows warm air from the rooms below to rise. This helps heat accumulation to dissipate during summer and serves as dead air insulation from cold winter air.

The simplicity of form is characteristic of the austere influence of German immigration to the Round Top area. Early settlers built homes pristine in form, mass, scale and used materials with simple detail. Later embellishments were added after success in farming and ranching provided surplus income.

URSULINE ACADEMY, 1852, 1854, 1870
San Antonio, Bexar County

From the *Texas Catalog, Historic American Buildings Survey:*
A small group of Ursuline nuns from New Orleans and Galveston arrived in San Antonio in September 1851 to found a school for girls which opened on November 3. The first academic building was completed in 1852 and is assumed to be the work of Jules Poinsard, a native of France who advertised himself as an architect and contractor experienced in pisé work—

rammed-earth construction. Later buildings are attributed to Fathers C.M. Dubuis in 1854 and Francis Giraud in 1870. The French origins of the nuns and their architects may have imparted some subtle French qualities to the construction.

Academy

Stuccoed pisé, 28 feet-6 inches by 80 feet, two stories, original hip roof now gabled, two-story galleries on long north and south sides, louvered shutters, bell cupola. Built 1851-1852 by Jules Poinsard.

Academy Building Addition

Limestone rubble, 68 feet by 45 feet, two stories with one-story wing, hip roof with tiny gabled dormers. Built in 1853-1854 and attributed to Father C.M. Dubuis.

Chapel

Limestone, 64 feet by 95 feet, cross surmounts gabled parapet, lancet-arched stained glass windows. The plan has a small nave, a large west transept with rear balcony and a very shallow two-story east transept or oratory. The tongue-and-groove ceiling dates from about 1900 and takes a gambrel form over the large transept and an inverted pyramid pendant at the crossing.

Dormitory

Limestone rubble, 46 feet by 152 feet, with west end cut obliquely to conform to the street, two stories, hip roof with square central clock tower with three clock faces and a blank north face, two-story gallery on north and east with square columns and ornamental box capitals. Begun in 1866 to provide housing for boarding students. Attributed to Francis Giraud.

Priest's House

Dressed limestone, 68 feet by 71 feet, two stories, gabled roofs with ornamental parapets at end walls, dormer faces are extensions of stone facade, sheet metal balustrade above cornice has repeated trefoil arch. Built about 1882-1885.

House

Limestone, 21 feet by 47 feet, two stories, gable roof, one-story porch at north. A plane house built in 1872 by John Campbell.

Laundry

Limestone, 70 feet by 40 feet, one and two stories, gable roof, one-story lean-to porches. The massing of these simple forms creates a complex of buildings carefully attached to assemble a heterogeneous grouping. The complex offers fine examples of the French architectural influence in a warm sunny climate.

The buildings are well protected from the sun, by the roof and porch overhangs, as are the windows by ventilating shutters. The porch rails, the evenly spaced columns on the

URSULINE ACADEMY *continued*

dormitory building and the academy building, additionally offer an order and visual rhythm to the faces of the structures. The uniformly symmetrical fenestration of the windows pro-

vide an additional order to the organization of the facades. The symmetry of the hipped and flared roofs contribute to the simple composition.

The stone mortar and rubble walls offer a texture to the facades. The cut-stone lintels, stone molding, and the stone sills above and below the windows of the academy building articulate the openings. The cut-stone gabled dormers with arched window openings, the cut-stone banister between the dormers and the dated pediment above the door suggest that an architect of some understanding designed these details to integrate with the mortar and rubble stone walls. The buildings were vacated in 1965 and the academy moved to a new location to provide for growth. The complex was later purchased by the City of San Antonio and over the years has been converted to an art academy and a private club. The chapel with the large open space has become an ideal facility for social gatherings and an assembly room. (See Department of the Interior, Paul Goeldner, compiler, Lucy Wheeler and S. Allen Chambers, Jr., eds., *Texas Catalog, Historic American Buildings Survey* [San Antonio: Trinity University Press, 1974], pp. 205-07.)

LIENDO, 1853

Hempsted vicinity, Waller County

The name "Liendo" is taken from the first land holder, Justo Liendo, who received a large land grant from the Mexican government. Leonard W. Groce paid $1,500 to Liendo for 3,000 acres of land in 1841 and became a cotton plantation owner with 1,000 slaves. The first bale of Texas cotton was produced on the Groce plantation. This framed two-story, fourteen-room house was built by Groce in 1853 of long-leaf Georgia yellow pine.

Liendo later became the home of the prominent German-born Texas sculptress, Elisabet Ney and her husband, Dr. Edmund Montgomery. They purchased it in 1873, along with 1,100 acres.

The house is a large two-story L-shaped plan, with a hipped roof and a Greek Revival portico. The form is simple. It is of domestic scale, although large, and only affordable by affluent Texans at the time of its construction and occupancy. The two-story front façade is handsomely designed with the portico well-proportioned to the entire form and is the most dominant element of the residence. The four square box columns with small square Doric capitals support the pediment and the second floor. In keeping with tradition, the front door is at the center axis of the façade, with a transom light and two side lights. In addition, the windows are symmetrically positioned at both levels around the front entrance. A traditional oval-shaped fan window is placed in the center of the pediment. The elliptical fan window is traditional in Greek Revival houses, but the half circle Roman fan window was also used in many houses of the period. This detail may be compared to the round Roman arch in the Stephen Blunt house or the flat Greek fan of the Ezekiel Cullen house, both in San Augustine.

PARSON ANDREW HERRON HOUSE, 1854

Seguin, Guadalupe County

The Herron home was built by pioneer Presbyterian minister Andrew Herron in 1854. This house is an uncomplicated two-story form with a gabled roof and portico entrance. Although it was constructed during the popular Greek Revival period, it appears to be a structure of native design. The adornments are minimal, and the fenestration and materials offer a statement of design solemnity—perhaps in keeping with austerity of the Presbyterian minister's faith. One of the fine visual qualities of the house is the sandstone ashlar stone masonry cut, shaped and laid by skilled masons. The symmetrical window and door fenestration on both levels and the projection of the two-story portico contribute to the unadorned aesthetic of the house. The double front door with flanking sidelights and overhead transom lights is a classical semblance that accents the entrance and contributes to the symmetry of the front elevation.

R.S. WILLIS HOUSE, 1854

Montgomery, Montgomery County

This structure has been maintained in excellent condition and appears to have had some additions and refinements incorporated over the years. Although the building was constructed when Greek Revival was popular, the characteristic adornments of that style are not obvious. Probably the original two-story gabled form, with windows uniformly and symmetrically spaced at the second floor, were different. The windows on the first floor are equally spaced and located but the front door is not positioned in the traditional central axis.

The Victorian-style columns and capitols suggest that the large one-story porch may have been added at a later time.

THE CEDARS [CAPTAIN ISAAC BAKER HOUSE], 1854-1860

Plantersville, Grimes County

Simple Greek Revival forms of this building have been expanded with a wing to the back of the house and a downstairs back porch. The portico is in keeping with the Texas traditions of the period. Plain two-story columns, with slight entasis and the Doric capitals, support the pediment and the second-floor porch. The treatment of the columns is not standard Doric order. A unique feature of the portico is the pilasters behind the columns which appear to support the architrave (the beam carrying the actual pediment, roof and ceiling). The pilasters, however, include rectangular capitals more in harmony with the Doric tradition. There is also a molded headboard scribed between the vertical pilasters and the horizontal siding above. The molding around the fascia, the pediment and the architrave is carefully mitered at the corners. The front doors at both levels are paneled and are flanked with sidelights.

No transom light appears above either door as so often is the tradition of the period.

The front windows—six-over-six panes—symmetrically flank the center axis of the front doors. Similar windows in the side wall are symmetrically located on either side of the chimney.

JOHN H. SEWARD HOUSE, 1855

Independence, Washington County

The John Seward House is a large residence that has been maintained by the same family since it was built. Although the house is modest with gabled roof unadorned by period embellishments, it has an elegance derived primarily from the six-bay double veranda along the full length of the front of the house. Evenly spaced columns and uniformity of the banister and palings present an orderly rhythm.

Framing and the exterior walls are cedar. A unique feature of the house is the separation of the roof from the walls and ceiling to compensate for the hot climate. A continuous opening, approximately one foot below the under side of the roof plate, extends across the entire front and the back of the house, allowing continuous ventilation in the attic. This ingenious detail prevents condensation under the roof and discourages moisture and dry rot.

WILLIAM L. CALLENDER HOUSE, 1855

Victoria, Victoria County

This house was built in 1854 by Dr. Stephen F. Cocke of pre-cut lumber ordered from the East. The Cocke family enjoyed an affluent and sophisticated lifestyle and an appreciation for architecture. The house was owned and occupied from 1854 to 1871 by attorney William L. Callender, who added a two-story wing at the back.

The house is uncomplicated and was designed and constructed in the Greek Revival tradition with a two-story raised first floor. The six symmetrically located square box columns supporting the veranda roof are uniformly spaced around the center axis. Each column has an applied Doric capital and a square base. The most unusual element of this façade is the crenated fascia beam that provides support for the porch roof. The porch banister rail and the palings offer an additional order to the rhythm of the column spacing.

The single front door has a transom light above and a classic pediment over the glass. Planed molding is applied to each door jamb. The windows at both the first and second floors are symmetrically located around the center axis. The first-floor windows have nine panes above and six below. The second floor windows are half frame, opened by sliding into the wall horizontally.

EARLE-HARRISON HOUSE, 1856-1858

Waco, McLennon County

The Earle-Harrison House was originally erected on an eleven-league grant conveyed to Thomas Jefferson Chambers by the Mexican states of Coahuila and Texas in 1832. Dr. and Mrs. Baylis Wood Earle acquired one-and-a-quarter acres of the land and began construction in 1858. The original house was half "Peristyle Greek" until money could be accumulated to complete the structure. Dr. Earle died before the second half of the house was finished. In 1872 the structure was purchased by

Mrs. Earle's brother, General Thomas Harrison. In 1986—threatened by an interstate highway project—it was moved to its present location and restored by architect Raiford Stripling under the auspices of the G. H. Pape Foundation.

This fine example of Greek Revival architecture was constructed by skilled craftsmen. Though the second half of the house was never completed, this Peristyle form is rarely found in Texas architecture of the period. The massing is quite simple: symmetrically placed Doric capitals and fluted columns (having correct entasis) sit on a non-traditional base. The floor-to-ceiling windows are symmetrically located on the façades but do not coincide with the column spacing. The entablature above the columns is well proportioned and the molding is cut and placed within in the traditions of the period. The double porch contributes to the fine scale and proportion. The siding is cypress; framing and flooring are heart pine and post oak. The columns were cut from cypress in East Texas and transported by oxen.

COCHERON MCDOWELL HOUSE, 1857

Bastrop, Bastrop County

The two-story Greek Revival Cocheron McDowell house, with shallow hipped roof and a two-story portico demonstrates a simple rectangular solid. The house has a large molded entablature extending around the entire roof and wall juncture. The four symmetrically spaced columns, two on each side of the entrance axis, offer classic adornment and support the balcony floor, the portico entablature and the roof. The square box columns are tapered to give the impression of entasis (usually found in round columns). Each column has a well-scaled, square Doric capital and a base traditionally not used with the Doric order. The balcony floor carries a molding—a traditional example of the classic period.

The two front doors, one on each level, accentuate the front entrance. The first-floor double doors incorporate traditional details of two flanking side lights and transom light. The fenestration of the front façade is resplendent with two large windows and shutters at each level symmetrically located on either side of the front doors. The left side wall, also with uniform fenestration, appears to have had one of the windows replaced by an exterior door.

WANTKE-POCHMANN SHOP AND HOUSE, CIRCA 1856
Round Top, Fayette County

This structure is reported to be one of the oldest buildings in Round Top (second only to the Schueddemagen House). Built about 1856 by a German settler as a shop for building pipe organs, it was later used as a home. The unadorned building is simply four walls covered by a gabled roof. There are two rooms on the ground floor and a loft above. The rubble masonry is carefully laid up plumb and true. Each window head is supported by a "jack arch," carrying the load of the stonework above the opening. The jack arch is derived from the round Roman arch; however, it is constructed as a flat lintel arch with stones slanting into a key stone (or center stone), locking the individual pieces together. The windows on the first floor are nine panes over six.

WESLEY BRETHREN CHURCH, 1866

Washington County

A small group of Czech settlers came to Washington and Austin counties during the early 1850s and were organized into a congregation by the Reverend Joseph Opocensky in 1864. The Wesley Brethren Church was built in 1866 and is considered the Mother Church of the Texas Brethren community.

The building is a single-room, one-story structure of wood. The plan is a simple and well proportioned rectangle for meet-ings with the length being approximately one third again the width. The steeply pitched gabled roof, a bell tower with a prominently steep spire, emphasizes a sense of verticality. The building is placed on shallow stone piers which preserve the integrity of the slightly rolling landscape and provide a sense of belonging to this site.

The fenestration is simple, with four evenly spaced, double-

WESLEY BRETHREN CHURCH *continued*

hung windows on the two side walls. The front elevation enestration is also symmetrical with a central double door (with panel inscription) and a transom fan light above and two small lancet-arched windows on either side. A small oculus is

centered immediately above the door near the top of the gable. Small rectangular louvered openings are located in the center of each face of the bell tower. An uncomplicated wood molding is placed at the top of the gabled façade and extends along the fascia at the roof eaves.

The interior of the church is painted with architectural ornamentation to symbolize brick. There are Ionic columns on pedestals between the windows, jack arch window heads and six pointed stars above each of the columns. An attempt is also made to create perspective: painted beams appear to span from the columns to the window heads. This Renaissance-style art was done by clergyman Bohuslav Emil Laciak in 1890.

The church has undergone several minor revisions and structural restorations over its life span; however, the integrity and concept of the building have been carefully retained.

FORT HOUSE, 1868

Waco, McLennan County

Most large houses in Waco were built as a product of the affluence created by King Cotton—the primary economic base of Texas before and, for many years after, the Civil War. Fortunes were made growing, processing and trading high quality cotton.

The Civil War essentially marked the end of the Greek Revival architectural period in America, although the Fort House—one of several in the Waco area designed with care, constructed by capable brick masons and carefully trimmed with precisely cut and planed wood trim—is a post-war structure.

The simple temple form and the similar configuration of the portico pediment create an unadorned massing, significant to the period. The pediment is supported by two fluted columns with subtle entasis, Ionic capitals and simple square bases. A small cantilevered balcony with a banister extends under the portico at the second-level door. The molding of the entablature, the fascia and the pediment are carefully shaped and installed. All corners are precisely mitered and trimmed, articulating the juncture of the masonry walls and the roof. The front doors at the first and second floors are located in the central axis of the façade but different in design. A transom light appears above both doors. The upper door has symmetrical side lights on either side, while the ground-level double door has no side lights but has an arch-topped window in each door. The masonry above the doors is supported by a white wood lintel that matches the white entrances while contrasting with the darker brick.

The windows are symmetrically located on either side of the front doors and are uniformly spaced in the side walls,

FORT HOUSE *continued*

giving an ordered composition to the façades. The window patterns are six-over-six lights with shutters. The arched brickwork and lintels over the windows are unique. The rowlock bond brick arch protrudes approximately one inch beyond the face of the wall, providing an "eyebrow" or a "hood" over each window. This feature directs rain water to the sides, rather than allowing water to drain over the window and trim.

CARL WILHELM RUMMEL HOUSE, CIRCA 1870

Round Top, Fayette County

The Carl Wilhelm Rummel house—a three-room plan of unadorned sandstone ashlar with a one-and-a-half story gabled roof and a single dormer—was built about 1870. At one time, the house was plastered over but the stonework on either of the side walls is revealed to expose the masonry. This is a fine example of the use of the available native materials, German cultural influence and inventive and ingenious craftsmanship. The overhanging veranda roof and the five uniformly spaced columns contribute to the pristine gracefulness of the house. The symmetrically located front doors, the two front windows and the similar side and back wall windows present a sophistication of design and uniformity of fenestration. The stone work, although not cut or shaped, is laid up with particular care. The shallow stone arches over the side wall windows exhibit the considerable craftsmanship that German settlers were well known for.

ANIMAL BARN AND CORN CRIB, THE LEWIS WAGNER FARMSTEAD, 1870
Winedale, Washington County

This barn was built in 1894 from cedar beams previously used in an 1850s-vintage cotton gin. The barn housed work animals, including mules, oxen and horses. Four log cribs inside the structure provided storage for shucked and unshucked corn.

The building is a fine example of a study in form, mass and space relations. The central two-story loft is surrounded on four sides by a one-story shed. Each form has a conspicuously different roof and rake, while the integrity of joining these forms into a single mass is accomplished with native sophistication. The design was created as one single entity to address the needs of the agrarian settlers.

The treatment of horizontal siding on the loft gables and roof shingles along with the vertical siding on the shed walls

creates a textural expression sympathetic to the form and function of the building.

The patterns of horizontal and vertical articulation for ventilation on the doors and adjoining walls are unique. Again, native sophistication has created a work of art in the delineation of the solids and voids.

IRISH FLATS

San Antonio, Bexar County

During the latter half of the nineteenth century, a large community of Irish immigrants arrived in Texas, moved to San Antonio and became part of the community. Most of the settlers established residences between North Alamo and Sixth streets, near downtown and within walking distance of their jobs.

Most of the houses of the Irish immigrants have been lost to development. Two, however, still stand and have been restored for new uses. Both houses are of modest scale; the sites are contiguous on the south side of Sixth Street.

Architectural form is simple. The smaller house is of stone bearing walls plastered inside and out, stone floor, gabled roof

with a rake break. The roof has a shallow pitch to cover the porch across the front and a different pitch to cover the salt box to the back. The fenestration, though simple, is pleasant in the symmetrical arrangement of the evenly spaced porch columns, the two uniformly spaced casement windows and the two doors. The porch roof columns have a tall base, trim at the corners, and a small capital at the top.

The slightly larger Victorian brick house is also simple in form with fenestration symmetrically arranged around the single front door. The main floor of the house is elevated a half level above grade and has a more steeply pitched roof. The roof is gabled with a modified hip on either end, a break at the upper roof eaves and a second rake covering the front porch and a room at the back. The window heads and the front door head are supported by a shallow round arch with brickwork forming an eyebrow. The most significant detail of the house is the circular wood and gingerbread spindles at the porch entrance creating an enticing Victorian pediment. It is supported by round columns with base and capital at the porch. The porch stairs and banister offer order to the front of the building. The top of the brick chimney was carefully laid with corbeled coursing, dentils and a wind and rain screen characteristic of the Victorian period.

THREE

TEXAS HILL COUNTRY

The Texas Hill Country is considered one of the most desirable areas in the state because of topography, climate, scenery and cultural heritage. One of the smallest regions in area, it includes Mason, Llano, Kimble, Gillespie, Blanco, Kendall, Hays, Comal, as well as parts of Bexar, Bandera and Medina counties.

The elevation ranges from approximately 1,000 to 2,000 feet above sea level, offering low humidity and comfortable temperatures. The winters are mild, the summers warm and the evenings cool. Most of the land encompasses plains, hills and some high plateaus. The bedrock is primarily limestone with area deposits of pink granite and sandstone. The soils are primarily reddish-brown to brown in color, neutral to slightly acid, gravelly, with stony sandy-loam. Trees such as juniper, oak, mesquite and cypress are found in the region. Short grass is also found.

It is frequently referred to as the German Hill Country in recognition of the immigrants who settled the area. Soon after Texas independence, a number of Germans came to the new Republic, but they found the coastal plain regions uncomfortable due to the high temperature and humidity. Many families moved to higher and dryer elevations. Settlers came from lower economic groups but were creative and highly industrious. For the first time in their lives, many became landholders. Their buildings were ingeniously designed and constructed using local stone and wood. Soon they introduced concepts of architecture and construction that they brought from their homeland. Artistic quality, structural integrity, articulation of fachwerk construction: cut stone, generous roof overhangs and porches became the hallmark of the finer German buildings.

In addition to German influences in the Hill Country, there are also examples of French architecture. The town of Castroville with the several smaller surrounding communities of D'Hannis, Vandenburg and Quihi, were named by French entrepreneur Henri Castro in 1844 and the Dutch financier (Vandenburg) who subsidized the transportation costs of the new settlers to Texas. Castro named streets of the community for family members, friends and capitols of Europe. Early settlers built log cabins, using the trees from along the Medina River as a source for timber. The weight and size of the logs required considerable manpower; thus, the settlers soon began building the traditional stone houses they had known in northern France. Stone provided better insulation, was more durable than wood, fireproof and offered an excellent defense against Indian attack. The stonemasons who settled in the Castroville area were accomplished craftsmen, skilled at stone cutting, stacking, jointing, quoining and in the use of stone lintels. Most stone houses were covered with a smooth coating of lime whitewash or plaster. (For more on Castroville, see O'Neil Ford, "Indigenous Architecture," *Southwest Review* [Vol. 19, No. 1]; Teresa Trawalter, *Henry Castro, A Study of Early Colonization in Texas*, Cornelia English Crook, ed. [San Antonio: St. Mary's University Press, 1988], p. 112.

Stone Construction (Quoining)

Alsatian House, Quihi, Medina County

This is a traditional example of Alsatian stone masonry. Through neglect and deterioration, much of the plaster has eroded, and the soft sand and lime mortar has worn away, leaving large cracks. The stone walls have not settled, but water erosion has caused joint openings to occur.

The exposed masonry exhibits several interesting features. The most prominent is the quoining at the corners that provides square and plumb angles. The large quoin stones were carefully shaped, squared, faced, and placed to interlock and give stability to the adjoining front and side masonry walls. Many of the stones are faced, and examination of the wall suggests that there was some effort at coursing. The walls appear to be twelve- to eighteen-inches thick and have remained in reasonably good condition for well over 100 years with little maintenance. This supports the idea that Alsatian masons were skilled craftsmen who had a clear knowledge of technology. Even with improved Portland cement mortar of today, it is unlikely that a modern mason could produce a wall of the same or better quality.

CORDIER-TSCHIRHART-SEAL HOUSE, 1844

Castroville, Medina County

Simplicity of form prevails throughout the Cordier-Tschirhart-Seal House through its solid rectangular form and traditional gabled roof. The location is practical in its orientation to the sun and prevailing breezes: the house faces south to capture the warmth and light of the sun during the winter months. A winter photograph shows bare trees, strong shade under the porch roof and sunlight on the unprotected portion of the front wall, illustrating the importance of the warmth and light during the cool, short days of this season.

Castroville, as a whole, is carefully laid out with the primary streets oriented to the east and west, providing the most desirable building façades to the gentler sun of the south and north. Accordingly, homes get maximum exposure to the low south winter sun. In addition, the overhanging porch roofs shelter the walls and windows from the strong high midday summer sun. Houses facing north on the opposite side of the street were frequently designed with back porches exposed to the south. The front and back porches received cool summer breezes and offered comfort to the residents. East and west walls received strong sun in the early morning and late evening and were built with minimal horizontal dimension for less solar exposure.

The Cordier-Tschirhart-Seal dwelling, one of the first in the community, has been altered to meet the needs of contemporary lifestyle and practical maintenance. The original, like all early Castroville houses, had a hand-split cedar or cypress shake roof, but that has been replaced with manufactured composition shingles. Also, the front porch roof has been rebuilt with modern machine shaped columns, modern fascia molding, and a stone porch floor not in keeping with the original settlers' notions. Regardless of these modifications, the edifice remains as an original Alsatian house of handsome proportions and configuration.

BOURQUIN HOUSE, 1844

Castroville, Medina County

Henri Castro probably also owned the land on which the Bourquin House is located. W. B. Patterson, a well-to-do settler and the Medina County district clerk, built the house sometime between 1844 and 1849 and owned the property until 1868.

That year Henry T. Renken, a prosperous farmer and rancher and an active member in the community, purchased the property, including the improvements, from the Patterson heirs for $400. Renken's widow lived in the house until her death in 1906, and her heirs kept the property until 1908 when they sold it to Mary J. Bendele. Anna Bourquin purchased the tract for $1,200 from Mrs. Bendele in 1928. Her family retained the house until the 1970s when Tom Messer and Fred Pottinger

BOURQUIN HOUSE *continued*

of San Antonio bought it to serve as their summer and week-end residence. They have restored the house.

The Bourquin house is a simple rectangular solid with a gabled roof and a flatter rake at the back over the salt box to reflect the Alsatian architecture of Castroville. The gallery at the front provides shade from the summer sun and diverts winter winds. The fenestration of the house is symmetrical around the center. Both the front and the back façades have two doors centrally balanced with two windows equally spaced on either side and uniformly and symmetrically spaced columns support the gallery.

The construction is stone covered with painted plaster. All the doors and windows are deeply set in thick stone walls. The eight windows are arranged in a six-over-six pane pattern. The dark trim openings contrast sharply. This is the only house in Castroville with six fireplaces.

THEODORE GENTILZ HOUSE, CIRCA 1846

Castroville, Medina County

The Theodore Gentilz house was built on one of the original lots granted to Gentilz by Henri Castro, who ordered the construction of this house at the same time as the construction of his own residence. Gentilz was an accomplished engineer and draftsman whose work included much of the planning and layout of Castroville and the surrounding communities. In addition, he was an accomplished artist and produced many of today's prized paintings of San Antonio and South Texas.

The house is of traditional Alsatian stone construction with a gabled roof over the two-story section and a flatter rake shed roof over the salt box. The faced masonry on the lower levels of the walls is made of carefully placed coursed larger stones. The upper levels of the masonry walls, which appear to be laid with smaller stones, are not as carefully coursed. The corners are laid with cut face stones and interlocked with the side and front walls by conventional quoining techniques.

Likely the exterior walls of the house were originally plastered or painted with lime whitewash.

The fenestration is simple; however, there was apparently no effort to compose the window and door openings in any pattern or symmetry. Traditional Alsatian houses had porches as a prominent part of the front façade. The Gentilz house, however, does not have a porch; it may never have had one or one may have been removed at a later date.

HENRI CASTRO HOMESTEAD, CIRCA 1846

Castroville, Medina County

This pristine white stone building with plastered walls is elegant both in its simple form and in the symmetry of the front façade fenestration. The two front doors and the three windows are spaced equally and offer a statement of order that portrays the builder's sensitivity to visual effect. The six columns supporting the outer edge of the porch roof are also spaced to coincide with the pattern of the doors and windows.

Many Alsatian houses have ground level porch floors made of stone pavers, while Anglo houses traditionally have elevated porch floors constructed of wood.

The generous overhang on the front of the house protects the outside wall, windows, and doors from heat and rain. The house roof is covered with cypress shingles and has a steep pitch and a lower rake over the porch and back of the structure. The traditional fireplace with an outside chimney is on the north side of the house; however, the south wall incorporates an inside chimney above the windows that suggests a stove was used to warm the interior.

An important feature of the typical Alsatian house is the sharp contrast between light and dark materials. The lime-plastered white walls give a distinct value contrast between the doors and windows, the shades and the shadows.

PRIVATE RESIDENCE
CLOSED TO PUBLIC

FIRST CATHOLIC CHURCH, 1847

Castroville, Medina County

Located on Anglo Street between Paris and London streets, this small single-room structure—eighteen-by-twenty-four feet—is constructed of local stone and plastered on the inside. The parish soon outgrew the space available for services, and a larger church was built in 1850. The church supports a gabled roof with a flat rake at each of the outer eaves. The stonework is of faced stones without coursing and with quoins at the corners locking the walls together.

The single, six-paneled entry door is flanked by rough cut jambs on either side and a similar wood head. The wood in this building is oak and cypress (see Homer H. Lansbury, delineator, "First Catholic Church" (TEX-359), in "Historic American Building Survey," September 9, 1936).

Ray Boehle Barn, circa 1850s
Quihi Road, Medina County

The Ray Boehle structure is called a barn; however, it is a more complex building than meets the eye, serving simultaneously as the homestead and the farmstead. As the stone facility is seriously deteriorating, it is likely to be lost unless it is considered for short-term preservation consolidation or closing in. Certainly it is a structure of cultural and historic significance and should be a candidate for acquisition and restoration by an appropriate organization.

The concept of combining the residence with the animal shelter may have been derived from the traditions of the European *parti*, where the family and the livestock were housed together for convenience, warmth and security. The building does stray from the traditional simplicity of mass. This edifice introduces three, rather than one, simple and well-defined forms: the longitudinal ground floor with the shallow symmetrically pitched gabled roof; the doubled height of the asymmetrically pitched roof in the stable and feed-storage area; and the second-floor rectangular solid form with a second symmetrically pitched gable roof. The ingenuity of combining these forms into a single integrated mass probably evolved from Old World experiences or observations. The product is a pleasing aesthetically ordered composition.

Unfortunately, the white plaster originally used on the interior and exterior walls has deteriorated. This must have been an attractive edifice in its original condition, displaying the play of light and shadow while integrating intricate massing of forms.

The planned opening between the residence and the animal areas was a functional decision. The opening through the building creates a void that punctuates the three forms where they are commonly joined and emphasizes the visual articulation of light, shade and shadow.

The building is located midway between Castroville and Quihi on an elevation that provides good drainage and a commanding view. The traditional north-south orientation gives the advantage of shade and cross ventilation. The open ports in the stable wall permit air to enter at lower levels as heat increases, causing the warm air to rise to the upper level and offer ventilation and cooling for the animals.

JOSEPH CARLE HOUSE, 1850S

Castroville, Medina County

The Carlé house at the corner of Madrid and Anglo Streets was built in the 1850s by Joseph Carlé and was used as a residence and store during the early part of the twentieth century.

The structure is built of native limestone, cypress, cottonwood and oak with walnut woodwork that reflects the Alsatian heritage and building technology of the period. The first floor has three rooms, a storeroom, a large hall and two porches on the rear. The second floor has four rooms, a hall and a balcony on the front supported by wrought iron brackets.

The form is a large, simple, two-story rectangular solid with a gabled roof over the middle and a front second floor balcony that extends beyond the front wall. The rear roof over the salt box assumes a slightly flatter rake. A one-story wing containing the kitchen and dining room is built on the back side of the house to form an "L" plan. The house is constructed of stone masonry with plastered walls inside and out. The fenestration of the front façade is symmetrical: the two first-floor doors are equally spaced and the single door on the second floor is centered with two flanking windows symmetrically placed and spaced.

An unusual second-floor balcony extends across the entire façade. Rounded metal brackets beneath the floor support the exterior edges, and the interior edges are anchored to the masonry wall. The balcony can only be gotten to from the second floor. The equal spacing of the balcony columns that support the outer edge of the roof emphasizes the symmetry. (See description by Homer H. Lansbury, January 19, 1937, "Historic American Buildings Survey" [TEX-390]. p. 69.)

LANDMARK INN AND OUTBUILDINGS, PORTIONS BUILT BEFORE 1853 [VANCE HOTEL]

Castroville, Medina County

About 1849, Cesar Monod purchased two lots in Castroville on which he built a structure where he lived and ran a general store. The building was a one-story, plastered-stone structure with a detached kitchen that resembled the Alsatian farmhouses in northeastern France.

In 1853 an Irish immigrant named John Vance bought the property and opened a general store. He added a second story and the first- and second-floor galleries. The well-known wagon stop was located on the heavily traveled route between San Antonio, El Paso and northern Mexico, so Vance frequently

LANDMARK INN AND OUTBUILDINGS {VANCE HOTEL} *continued*

rented rooms and furnished supplies to travelers, including military visitors. Soon the building was known as the Vance Hotel.

Vance built a story-and-a-half residence for his family and a two-story bathhouse between the inn and the Medina River. According to legend, the lead lined water tank on the second floor of the bathhouse was melted down to cast bullets and mini-balls during the Civil War.

In 1854, Vance sold a portion of his property to George L. Haass and Laurent Quiontle, who added a stone gristmill and a wood and stone dam across the river to provide water and power.

Jordan T. Lawler purchased the mill, the inn and the Vance

residence in 1925 and reopened the hotel as the Landmark Inn, which became widely known as a peaceful oasis.

The Landmark Inn and associated buildings are architecturally unique to the region. The main building dates from 1853 and is little changed since the second story was added in 1874. The Texas Parks and Wildlife Department restored it to its present state in the 1940s and presently operates it as a hotel.

Like many historic buildings of the period, the inn is simple with a one-story wing perpendicular to the primary two-story structure. When visualized as a whole, the individual forms offer a simplicity in massing. Five rhythmically and sym-

metrically spaced square wood columns support the two-story gallery and carry the load of the porch, the second-level porch floor, the roof and the exterior stair. The doors and windows of the façade are uniformly placed to offer a composition of visual order and interest.

The broken roof line at the transition between the solid white plastered stone end wall and the depth of the open gallery create a shallow roof rake over the gallery that suggests a counterpoint in the form of the building by emphasizing the solid and the void of the elevation.

LANDMARK INN AND OUTBUILDINGS {VANCE HOTEL} *continued*

The white plaster over the stone walls in concert with the white wood gallery and columns create a sharp contrast of shade and shadow from the direct light of the morning sun. The rhythm of the vertical and horizontal surfaces, accenting the feeling of order, appears uniformly through the dark and light values. The handrail, the evenly spaced palings on the second floor gallery and the exterior stair give unique detailed features to the façade.

The stone bathhouse is a simple square two-story structure with a hipped roof, a door on the first floor, a door at the second level approached by a stair and a balcony at the opposite end of the upper floor. The masonry is laid faced stone and the corners are quoined to lock the walls together. There is an attempt at coursing the masonry by inserting ports on the second floor to allow joists.

The mill is an unadorned rectangular cube with a gabled roof and single window and door openings, offering a specific penetration in visual order. The stone work is of mortar and rubble with face stones incorporated; however, there appears to be no attempt at coursing the masonry.

THE KIEFER HOUSE, 1870

Castroville, Medina County

In 1870 Blaise Kiefer, a French immigrant, contracted with Joseph Schorpe, Sr., to design and build this home on the property adjoining his saloon and brewery. Kiefer established the first brewery in Texas in the cellar of the building.

The strong Creole-French influence seen in the house reflects the time Schorpe spent in New Orleans. It is not a true Alsatian-style house; it more closely resembles the "raised cottage-style plantation homes" of Louisiana, evidenced in the long flight of entrance stairs at the front that leads to the second-floor gallery. The iron stair railing was brought from New Orleans when the house was under construction. The upper gallery entrance leads to the formal rooms, and each room has six-and-one-half-foot French windows to the front and back and a separate entrance from the front gallery. The original house—designed to catch the prevailing breezes from the south—was only one room deep.

The front gallery is carved from the rectangular solid form, respecting the integrity of the simple configuration. The slop-ing seam metal roof with a flatter rake over the porch and front of the house provides a break in the roof plane. The placement of the windows, doors, porch columns and the pales and handrail of the gallery banister provides order to the front façade. (See "Castroville Pioneer Homes Pilgrimage 1982" [Castroville: Castroville Garden Club].)

AUGUST FALTINE HOUSE, 1845

Comfort, Kendall County

The August Faltine House is believed to be the oldest structure on its original site in Comfort. Fritz and Theodore Goldbeck built the log house of cypress in 1854, and it served as Comfort's first mercantile establishment. August Faltine purchased the dwelling in 1856 and added the traditional German fachwerk. The house was restored during the 1980s by great-grandson, August Faltine.

The restoration includes a salt box to the rear and the end of the log house. The porch extends the total length of the house, and the roof is steep at the gable and has a change of slope with a flatter rake over the salt box and the porch. The vertical and horizontal timber fachwerk construction supports the roof using diagonal bracing within the frame introduced to counter racking. The timber frame is infilled with cut stone, neatly faced and coursed, to provide an aesthetic design for the exterior walls. The fachwerk was originally plastered over to provide a uniform visual appearance and to offer additional resistance to water penetration. More recently, the original plaster was removed from the exterior walls to expose the stone. The interior walls, however, remain plastered today.

FERDINAND LINDHEIMER HOUSE, CIRCA 1852

New Braunfels, Comal County

Ferdinand Jacob Lindheimer, a German immigrant from Frankfurt am Main, unlike many early German settlers in Texas, had a sound education in mathematics and classical languages. He migrated to Texas in 1836 because of political oppression in Frankfurt and participated in the Texas Revolution soon after his arrival. Lindheimer was also a botanist and Texas offered an opportunity to research previously unidentified plants. Collecting trips kept him in the field for months at a time and through his dedication and research, Lindheimer was known as the "Father of Texas Botany." In 1852, Lindheimer terminated his botanical research and became editor of the *Neu-Braunfelser Zeitung*, which was published in his house for twenty years.

The house is presently the property of the New Braunfels Conservation Society. The original section was built in 1852 and restored in 1967. It is modest in size and unadorned in the austere style of the Teutonic settlers. Orinally, the house was one story constructed of traditional half-timber framing with plastered brick nogging between the timber frame. A sharply pitched gabled roof covers the dwelling and the front porch. Horizontal clapboard wood siding closes the left gable and four symmetrically spaced columns support the front porch roof. The window pattern uses nine-over-six panes. A later addition to the back uses exposed fachwerk framing with stone nogging and a flatter raked roof.

MAJOR EDWARD BURLESON HOUSE, CIRCA 1850S

San Marcos, Hays County

Edward Burleson, Jr., was born in Tennessee, the eldest son of the Texas revolutionary hero General Edward Burleson. He came with his parents to San Marcos in 1831, served with distinction in the Mexican War and reached the rank of major during the Civil War.

The unrestored house has been maintained in excellent condition. It was built during the Greek Revival period and exhibits many of the elements and details unique to the era. The temple form of the house, attached two-story gallery, four symmetrically spaced square wood columns and molded wood capitals at the top are significant icons of Greek Revival design. Some features, however, including the stone wings attached to the brick central portion, may have been added at a later date to give some embellishment to the plain façade of the original brick edifice. In addition, the palings and handrail at the upper level of the gallery, likely from the Victorian period, give a rhythmic and pleasing composition of vertical and horizontal elements.

The brick masonry exterior and interior walls of the second-story portion of the house and the first-story stone rooms are eighteen inches thick.

FRENCH LEGATION, 1841

Austin, Travis County

The French Legation in Austin was founded in 1839 at the request of Republic of Texas President Sam Houston.

French diplomat Jean Pierre Isidore Alphonse Dubois traveled to Texas to assess the new nation and visited Galveston, Houston and Matagorda. His favorable reports shaped France's recognition of the Republic.

Dubois returned to Texas in 1840 and declared himself the charge d'affaires. He traveled to Austin, the new capitol named

FRENCH LEGATION *continued*

for patron Stephen Fuller Austin, and searched the area for a place to build his home. He settled on property east of Austin, overlooking the Colorado River.

The style of the small frame house was influenced by the architecture introduced to Louisiana from French colonies in the Carribbean. Constructed of Bastrop pine, it displays many unusual characteristics. The house has a hipped roof, French doors that open onto a well-proportioned Louisiana porch and paired columns that face south towards the river. Light shines through dormer windows to illuminate the attic space on the upper level and a wine cellar occupies the area beneath the central hallway.

The framework exhibits fine craftsmanship and the foundation frame is composed of hand-adzed oak and juniper timber, squared and connected with chiseled joints and wood pegs. The wood probably came from the original site.

In 1934 the Works Progress Administration Historic American Buildings Survey undertook a review of the property; however, it mistakenly reversed the sites of the original kitchen and privy. The State of Texas purchased the property in 1948 and assigned custodial care to the Daughters of the Republic of Texas (DRT). In 1955 that organization asked Raiford Stripling to study the site and restore the house. Stripling

correctly identified the original locations of the outbuildings and, in several phases, the house and surroundings were restored to the original condition. (See Michael McCullar, *Restoring Texas: Raiford Stripling's Life and Architecture* [College Station: Texas A&M University Press, 1985], pp. 129-30.)

The French Colonial style was modified for the warm Texas environment: the front, facing south, is well protected from the summer sun and shaded by a large gallery roof. The generous window openings on each façade allow good ventilation.

Double columns support the roof, and the six pairs of square wood columns with molded wood capitals are equally spaced and symmetrically located across the front of the gallery, giving rhythm and order to the front. The double entrance doors, floor to ceiling windows and the smaller windows beyond symmetrically flank the door and enforce visual order to the house. The banister above and the three symmetrically placed dormers on the roof offer an order to the façade.

The rectangular solid of the house with the hipped roof and gallery offers the simplicity of form that dominated and accented early architecture of the period. The white siding offers a contrast between the shadows of the house forms, the dark doors and window openings and the shuttered covers.

GOVERNOR'S MANSION, 1853–1855

Austin, Travis County

This building is an excellent example of Texas architecture and, according to the National Register of Historic Places Inventory, it is one of the few Greek Revival governors' mansions still in use. Located on a hill southwest of the capitol, the mansion is a symmetrical two-story residence with a flat roof. The north side is stuccoed brick painted white; the remainder is exposed and painted brick. The two-story front gallery has five bay insets. Fluted wood columns with Ionic capitals, entablature with dentils and the wide cornice classify this as an Ionic structure. The absence of a pediment reflects a regional architectural characteristic.

The second-story gallery is full width and incorporates a graceful and delicate wood balustrade introduced by Austin master builder Abner Cook. This design assembles slender slats together to form an open diamond pattern known as crowfoot balusters. The balustrade and stair railing on the first floor is a modern addition.

Traditional details characteristic of Cook's Greek buildings are the sidelights and the unusually tall transom beside and over the front door. The pilasters flanking the door jambs carry a high entablature and intersect the transom. There are five-over-six-pane sash windows with shutters on the second story and floor-length six-over-nine-pane sashes on the first floor gallery.

Additions were made to the original block of the separate Victorian carriage house including a modified mansard roof. Walls, terracing and gardens were added during John Connally's residence in the early 1960s.

CARRINGTON-COVERT HOUSE, 1853-1857

Austin, Travis County

The Carrington-Covert House, dating back to the 1850s, is one of few historic houses still located on state property. The house is noted for its fine stonework that includes two street façades constructed of cut stone, corners articulated by quoining and jack arches serving as lintels above the windows. The restored building currently houses the Texas Historical Commission and is listed in the National Registry of Historic Places Inventory.

In 1852, a successful merchant named Leonidas Davis Carrington came to Austin, opened a store and began to purchase land in and around Austin. Within a few years, Carrington had become wealthy through land speculation. In 1853 he purchased a lot north of the capitol from Captain James M.W. Hall for $1,000. He bought building materials from 1853 to 1857 and pursued the construction of his home to completion during those four years.

Carrington sold the house and the land to M.L. Hemphill of Bastrop on May 5, 1870. Later Mr. and Mrs. Frank M. Covert bought the house and remodeled it. Covert sold the house on September 17, 1944, for $18,500. In 1968 a state agency bought the house and planned to tear it down to make room for a new building; protests and telegrams postponed the destruction, however, until the Texas legislature could pass a bill to protect the property.

The two-story dwelling has twenty-inch-thick limestone walls that were probably quarried from Comal Bluff. It contains twelve rooms, two large halls and floors constructed of wide heart-pine boards. The "L" shape is barely set back from the property line with the front façade and front door facing the street. The double gallery on the inside of the "L" offers a visual depth to this elevation. The banister palings, rails, gallery stair and slender wood columns offer an ordered composition. The windows are equally spaced and accented by shutters with each window sash having a four-over-four composition.

ST. DOMINIC CHURCH, 1853 AND 1868

D'Hanis, Medina County

D'Hanis, today identified as Old D'Hanis (a more recent community developed at a different location after the coming of the railroad in 1881), is one of the four satellite communities that Henri Castro established in the vicinity of Castroville. During 1846 and 1847, Theodore Gentilz and party planned and staked out the new community and the family plats where newcomers might establish homesteads. During the spring of 1847, the first twenty-nine families arrived and set about building temporary homes. The settlers met with extreme and extensive privations, including Indian raids, lack of food, few guns, shortage of ammu-

nition, epidemics of cholera and other diseases, lack of medical services, language difficutlies among others.

The first D'Hanis church and school—initially served by clergy from Castroville—was a log structure. In 1853 the community became a mission parish and the Reverend Dominic Mesens, O.M.C., was appointed the first pastor. Father Mesens directed the erection of a small two-story stone church that later was expanded into the larger 1868 structure by attaching the new nave to the west face of the original building. It is thought that the parishioners named their church for the patron Saint Dominic, as well as for Father Dominic.

The Gothic building—abandoned after 1915 following a devastating fire—today stands in stone ruins. The flames consumed the wood roof and bell tower, causing the parishoners to move to the present Holy Cross Church in D'Hanis. The architecture of the original structure is simple in form and detail, with stone walls supported by stepped buttresses, Gothic lancet windows and door, and, prior to the fire, a gabled roof. Two opposing stone lintels are laid diagonally creating a pointed

arch and emulate the lancet arch at the head of the door and the windows.

The stone work at the corners and at the buttresses was carefully quoined with cut stone, giving the walls stability by dovetailing the stones together and locking the masonry securely. The construction, laid up by accomplished masons, has proven to be solid and substantial and is confirmed by the structural integrity of the plumb walls over a hundred years after creation.

The bell tower was constructed of wood and fit into the rectangular notch in the masonry wall over the front door. Two bells in the tower tolled for the functions of the parish.

SAINT LOUIS CHURCH, 1868–1870

Castroville, Medina County

This is the third St. Louis Church in Castroville, the two pre-ceding structures having been outgrown by the expansion of the parish as it matured. The second church is no longer standing. The second parish building, though much smaller, appears from the photographs to have been similar to the pres-ent church in form and in detail. Father Peter Richard from Loire, France, is primarily responsible for having gained per-mission to build the church and to oversee its construction. Most of the labor was furnished by men of the parish. The stained glass windows were produced in Europe and in the United States. The structure is constructed of local stone, faced and carefully laid with consistent coursing. In 1870, the cost to build the church was $35,000.

The church is an excellent example of Gothic Revival architecture; easily identified by the lancet-arch doors and windows. The vertical elements are emphasized by Gothic accents, including the elongated windows and pointed lancet arches, the tall bell tower (with the steep intonation spire and cross at the top), the uniformly spaced buttresses supporting the side walls, emphasizing the cadence with a window between each. The plan is the traditional nave, narthex and apse at opposite ends; there is, however, no transept, as is the frequent custom in the liturgical plan of Gothic churches.

FOUR

WEST TEXAS PLAINS

This vast region was essentially ranch country where all functions revolved around the development, maintenance and marketing of cattle. The original population of the region was derived from East Texas and included some plantation aristocracy frequently accompanied by their African American servants. Much of the settlement, however, was composed of poor whites and a few free blacks. John Chisum was the first large-scale rancher in the region, assembling a herd of some 10,000 cattle and establishing cow camps along the Concho River near its confluence with the Colorado in approximately 1863. Chisum, a native of Tennessee, ranched the area for approximately ten years and provided large supplies of beef to the Confederate army and later to markets in New Mexico.

Richard Coffey, another early rancher in the area, moved his residence and ranch headquarters several times. In 1862 he built "Picketville," a heavily stockaded village in Runnels County, for protection against hostile Comanches and Lipan Apaches. Later he took up residence in Concho County. Even though the army occupied a string of forts across Texas to protect settlers and their property, on one cattle drive Indian raiders claimed 1,010 head of cattle and fifty horses. The Comanches killed two men and wounded several drovers, including one of the Coffey sons. Six months later, Indians stole the remaining cattle and milk cows.

Slowly, though, Anglos and Germans rugged enough to survive the privations of hostile land and Indian raiders settled West Texas.

The physiography of the West Texas High Plains is unique to the five recognized regions; it is composed primarily of irregular plains, some with hills and tablelands. Elevations range from 250 feet to over 3,000 feet above sea level. Geologic ages vary with areas that are from the Quaternary, Pliocene, Miocene, Oligocene, Cretaceous, Jurassic, Triassic and Permian periods. Vegetation includes plains grassland, mesquite savanna, juniper oak, and desert scrub savanna.

The rivers, though smaller than East Texas streams, flow in a similar pattern from east to west. A major fresh-water aquifer, a primary resource for today's agricultural communities, is the Ogallala formation. Minor aquifers include the Trinity and the Santa Rosa sands.

Mean dates of first frosts range between November 1 and November 16. The last sub-freezing temperatures are between March 31 and April 16. Mean annual temperatures extend from 56 to 68 degrees, and the mean length of the warm season is from 185 to 275 days per year. The mean annual relative humidity ranges from 39 percent to 75 percent; the mean annual precipitation varies from 8 inches to 28 inches per year, the extreme western areas being the driest. The mean annual possible days of sunshine ranges from 70 to 80 percent per year, the western areas receiving the most sunny days.

One of the earliest forms of housing was the half-dugout, a shelter dug into a hillside, roofed with sod and fronted with wood or stone. Although earth-embedded buildings have been constructed throughout history, this particular design was especially useful in the arid plains where earth and stone building materials were readily available and trees were scarce. Because the dugout captured the warmth of the earth in winter and its coolness in summer, comfortable temperatures were more easily and economically maintained in these dwellings. These structures were practical because they used available materials and made the most of the limited skills of local laborers. Later, as sawn timber was transported into these areas, half-dugout construction was used only for outbuildings.

Where timber was available, some log construction was used. In fact, most of the early stone and earth structures were quickly superseded by sawn timber shipped from East Texas, producing an abundance of frame houses and farmstead structures. There was little emphasis on using the Classical orders in the architecture; however, after the turn of the century, Victorian designs came into prominence.

Dugout Construction

*Lem Creswell Half-Dugout,
circa 1900, Concho County*

The Lem Creswell half-dugout is located on a narrow shelf overlooking the Colorado River. The original house has undergone many modifications and additions over several decades; these changes explain the partial dug-out and the limited above-grade structure. The building is an organic dwelling built of random native masonry. "V"-crimped galvanized sheet metal supported by masonry walls and wood posts taken from local trees covers the shallow, sloping roof. The building massing is complex due to expansions and additions.

Initially these buildings were simple excavations, but they evolved into shelters totally below grade with openings emerging only underground and a simple wood covering sometimes topped with soil. Later, as additional materials including stone and wood were combined with local technology, the half-dugout became an outgrowth.

photos courtesy Joe and Martha Freeman (author's collection)

The Ranching Heritage Center

Lubbock, Lubbock County

The Ranching Heritage Center was made possible by a private grant for the preservation of the legacy of the late-nineteenth and early-twentieth century Texas ranching industry. The focus is on locating, researching the origins, collecting, reassembling and accurately restoring original and exemplary building types. This project was assigned to the Texas Tech University at Lubbock, the institution traditionally associated with West Texas cattle and agricultural industries.

The earth structures on display are primarily indigenous to West Texas.

EL CAPOTE CABIN, CIRCA 1838

Ranching Heritage Center, Lubbock County

This cabin from the El Capote Ranch headquarters is a primitive log structure and was built in about 1838. It is a classic example of round log with double saddle-notch joint construction. Chinking is of wood, rocks and earth. The roof shakes are hand split and nailed into round wood rafters and purlins. The only prepared materials besides the basic ax-cut logs are the wood planks for the doors, shutters and the board-and-batten gable walls. The boards were hand hewn with an adz to a rough thickness and then hand planed to the finished thickness.

The mud cat (or "pen") chimney is rarely seen today other than in restorations because the mud quickly erodes from the rare rains and dampness rising from the earth. In low rainfall regions such as the West Texas Plains, mud chimneys survive well. The house logs are cut away at the stone fireplace so that the chimney could be attached to the firebox in the house.

HEDWIG HILL CABIN, CIRCA MID-1850S
Ranching Heritage Center, Lubbock County

The log house was originally located overlooking the Llano River, nine miles southeast of Mason in Mason County. Little is known of the history of the dwelling.

The building is constructed of carefully shaped and joined stone, has a shake roof and appears to be of sophisticated masonry technology.

JOWELL RANCH STONE HOUSE, CIRCA 1875

Ranching Heritage Center, Lubbock County

This building, a two-story stone residence with an accompanying outbuilding, was originally located near the south shore of present-day Possum Kingdom Lake, thirteen miles northwest of Palo Pinto. Legend claims that the resident, George Jowell, returned from a cattle drive and found his house burned to the ground. Consequently, he constructed this stone building to withstand the raids of the Comanche and Kiowa.

The masonry is laid as coursed faced stones with quoins at the corners for interlocking the construction. Cut and faced stone lintels support the window and door heads. The building is pleasantly articulated by its simple form with a chimney interrupting the plane of the end wall. The window and door openings punctuate the surface of the side wall, and the exterior stair adds a visual element to the simplicity of the building. The root, vegetable and fruit cooling storage house, is a small stone building with a shallow curved arch that supports the door head. The storage house is positioned to illustrate the pleasing relation between the two structures.

photos courtesy Joe and Martha Freeman (author's collection)

MASTERSON ROCK BUNKHOUSE, CIRCA 1879

Ranching Heritage Center, Lubbock County

The original location of this bunkhouse was fifteen miles west of Truscott in King County. The building was constructed about 1879 using coursed limestone for the walls and chimney. The wood-shingle gabled roof was extended to cover the porch in front and to give a break in the rake of the roof. The gabled end walls are closed with traditional boards and battens. The simplicity of form is obvious; however, the break in the porch shed roof and the change of the roof rake suggests a sensitive consideration in the visual composition of form. The scale of the building is pleasantly modest, suggesting its domestic function.

BAREFIELD SCHOOLHOUSE, CIRCA 1880S

Ranching Heritage Center, Lubbock County

The Barefield Schoolhouse was originally located on Farm Road 262, one mile southwest of Clarendon in Donley County. It is a one-room school typical of early rural educational facilities of the ranch country. This building, probably built in the 1890s, is constructed from the sawn timber, signifying late construction in the high plains region. Horizontal siding is applied over vertical strip board-and-batten construction. Cedar posts are driven into the earth at all four corners.

The building is a simple basic form composed of a gabled roof atop a rectangular solid. The corners are articulated by vertical corner boards, providing a visual terminus for the horizontal siding and adding diagonal and vertical stability in case of high winds, preventing air and dust infiltration and

providing a solid surface for attaching the building to the cedar anchor posts. The walls are infilled with horizontal siding with simple windows in the side walls and a door in the end wall.

HARRELL HOUSE, CIRCA 1883, 1899–1913
Ranching Heritage Center, Lubbock County

The Harrell House was originally located in Scurry County, north of Snyder. This home was expanded to meet the demands of family growth as additional resources became available. The original house was built of stone with board-and-batten additions in 1883; the first box-and-strip addition was made in 1899.

Remaining additions were added between 1899 and 1913.

The gable roof of the house and shed roofs on the porches give a homogeneous series of forms by adding carefully related forms, slopes, materials and details without disturbing the unity of the structure.

LAS ESCARBADAS, CIRCA 1886

Ranching Heritage Center, Lubbock County

The XIT Ranch in Deaf Smith County was at one time the largest spread under fence in Texas with seven divisions and 3,000,000 acres of land. This land once belonged to the State of Texas but was deeded to the contractor of the state capitol building in exchange for his services.

This headquarters building is a large structure of simple form. It has a gabled roof, long verandah across the front, symmetrically located doors and windows on the first and second floors, cut-and-faced-stone bearing walls and chimneys at both ends. The walls are carefully tied together at the corners with quoins. Instead of traditional masonry jack arches or stone lintels, wood frames support the heads above the doors and windows.

MATADOR HALF-DUGOUT, 1891
Ranching Heritage Center, Lubbock County

The original site of the Matador half-dugout was in Dickens County sixteen miles northeast of Dickens. The architectural features illustrate the simplicity and economy of the construction. The building is on a modest scale with a simple form and few embellishments. The logs are notched, the roof shakes are split and the stone is laid uncut. This truly illustrates the use of limited technology and available materials.

"LONG S" BOX AND STRIP HOUSE, CIRCA 1903–1904

Ranching Heritage Center, Lubbock County

Charles A. Goldsmith built this house southwest of Patricia in Martin County of box and board-and-batten strip-sawn timber frequently referred to in the eastern states as "Jenny Linn." Such construction is accomplished by nailing vertical siding to the floor sill plate and the ceiling header then covering the joints between the boards with narrow battens to keep out rain, dust and wind. The skin becomes the bearing wall and no studs are erected as a structural frame, thus conserving wall space. This single-board wall provides the finished surface of the outside and the inside of the building. A disadvantage of this construction is that there is only the thickness of the boards and no depth for air space or insulation.

This residence is one story with a gabled roof, shed, front porch and a rear lean-to. The house has two front doors providing separate access to the symmetrically placed four rooms. The pure simplicity of this form and its fundamental construction give a modest elegance. The box-and-strip construction offers a scale and texture to the building. This house provides a sense of place and of belonging in the West Texas Plains.

THE STONE RANCH, LAMBSHEAD RANCH, 1856

Shackelford County

Newton C. Givens, a captain in the Second U.S. Dragoons, established Lambshead in 1856 as a homestead and a place of livelihood. He named the ranch after Thomas Lambshead, an early English settler. John Matthews, along with George and William Reynolds, acquired the collective ranch lands between 1870 and 1909. Descendents still operate a cattle ranch in the area.

The stone work is somber mortar and rubble masonry with a single central door and two small symmetrically placed windows equidistant from the door. The stone building provided protection from the elements and local intruders.

The two stone chimneys at the ends of the house vented the fireplaces. The building illustrates the simple austere lifestyle that was totally self-sustaining.

BILL McCAULEY HOUSE, CIRCA 1875–1886

Coleman County

The Bill McCauley house was constructed by a local cowboy, who learned the building trades while working for several cattle ranchers in the area. The house has been owned by various descendants of the William H. and Mabel Doss Day family and has been occupied since its completion.

The house is a salt-box form built of cut, faced and regularly sized local stone with joints fitted with somewhat loosely coursed lime and sand mortar. The foundation stones rise three courses above grade and extend approximately two to three inches beyond the face of the walls above. The front porch roof repeats the salt box form and is supported by four symmetrically spaced square wood columns.

The simplicity of this house and the stone masonry of the chimney and the footing walls are its greatest architectural features.

courtesy Joe and Martha Freeman (author's collection)

RICH COFFEY HOUSE, CIRCA 1880-1881
Concho County

The Rich Coffey house is constructed of simple indigenous forms, using local materials and built with a sensitivity to craftsmanship. The unadorned gabled façade has four windows symmetrically placed on either side of the central fireplace and chimney.

courtesy Joe and Martha Freeman (author's collection)

The house has an enclosed dog run with a single room on either side on both the first and the second floors. Each first-floor room has a stone fireplace and exterior chimney. The floors on both levels and on the porch are wood planking. The stair is located in the dog run and extends to the enclosed porch that continues along the south face of the house and offers exterior shelter and ventilation.

The most interesting feature of the structure is the carefully cut and squared face stones laid in regular courses with a semi-stretcher bond similar to the traditional brickwork stretcher bond. The masonry is exceptionally well crafted and remains in place as originally laid. Jonathan Cook, a skilled stone mason, is responsible for the workmanship that has insured the longevity of the building. The jack arches above the windows and doors are particularly interesting, as are the cut stone slabs at the sills.

CRESWELL-ROZZLLE HOUSE, 1880-1893

Concho County

This late Victorian house, built in 1880 and expanded in 1893, has several identifying features. The complex gabled roof, narrow window and door fenestration, and carefully cut and faced stone jambs, sills and lintels around the doors and windows demarcate the façade. The tall, narrow windows and doors accent the vertical emphasis introduced by the two stories and the steeply pitched seven gabled roofs.

The stone mason was a capable craftsman judging by the careful facing of the stones, the regular coursing of similar sized stones and the simple quions that lock the precise vertical corners together.

The roof forms and the roof junctures at the valleys and overhangs are of interest. The building suggests a more sophisticated concept than typical ranch houses of the West Texas Plains.

courtesy Joe and Martha Freeman (author's collection)

courtesy Joe and Martha Freeman (author's collection)

McLaine-Hafner House, circa 1885-1886

Concho County

William J. McLaine constructed the McLaine-Hafner House in about 1885 and 1886. It stands as an example of the late Victorian architecture of the West Texas Plains. The house is a simple two-story form with a gabled roof and two eyebrow dormers interrupting the fascia and the front roof. The stone is carefully cut and faced to a standard size with stone lintels and sills above and below the window openings. The joints are of sandy low lime mortar that has been raised and scored. The porches were added at a later date.

Of interest is the board-and-batten gabled-roof outbuilding with a central chimney, two doors and a window. This building was attached to the stone house, but later it was moved.

LEADAY SCHOOLHOUSE, CIRCA 1900

Coleman County

This simple frame building has a hipped roof and portico and stands as the remaining landmark of what was once a plotted Coleman County town with a population of 100 persons. It is interesting to note that Leaday was founded by Rich Coffey.

This austere building might be seen as the most straightforward concept for a Texas Plains structure since it serves as a shelter for school-children in an isolated rural environment.

courtesy Joe and Martha Freeman (author's collection)

JOHN H. AND SARAH E. RANSBARGER HOUSE, DATE UNKNOWN

Runnels County

The Ransbarger house has many qualities in common with the Rich Coffey house. Jonathan Cook, a capable stonemason and the builder of the Coffey house, probably built the Ransbarger house. The uncomplicated configuration is similar to that of the Coffey house, the stonework is nearly identical, the fenestration is related and the stone details are entirely sympathetic.

A subtle difference in the stonework is the use of shallow rounded masonry arches rather than the flat jack arches at the window and door heads of the Coffey house.

Architecturally this house is a typical nineteenth-century ranch house with the heavy stone walls, simple forms and uncomplicated stone detailing that is sympathetic to the region.

courtesy Joe and Martha Freeman (author's collection)

OLD VOSS HOTEL, 1904

Voss, vicinity of Leaday, Coleman County

Mabel Doss Day Lea built this hotel at Voss to accommodate overnight travelers en route to and from Leaday and other West Texas communities. The somber, unadorned building is a rectangular cube with a gabled roof. A front porch across the entire façade offers an elegant pattern in light and shade. The unevenly spaced wood colonnade supporting the porch roof and the board-and-batten vertical siding suggest a visual rhythm. The fenestration has little relationship in terms of spacing or order with the window and door openings and the porch columns. Nevertheless, despite the lack of order, there is composition that has a certain visual attraction.

courtesy Joe and Martha Freeman (author's collection)

THE MABEL DOSS DAY LEA RANCH OFFICE, DATE UNKNOWN

Concho County

Although the date of this ranch office is unknown, it was likely built about 1905. All ranch business was conducted from this small, unadorned building.

The austerity of life and daily activities on the ranch is suggested by the modest architecture. This elegant, simple, small-scale one-story stuccoed building has two rooms, a steeply pitched gabled roof and a small porch sheltering the entrance.

FIVE

THE RIO GRANDE WATERSHED AND THE SOUTH TEXAS VALLEY

From its headwaters in Colorado, the Great River flows south through New Mexico, then runs southeast from El Paso to the Gulf of Mexico, forming the international border between Mexico and the United States. The lower valley ranges from Laredo to the Gulf while the upper watershed is identified as the vast region between Laredo and El Paso. At the fertile eastern delta topographical forms include flat plains bordering the Gulf and rising to approximately 250 feet above sea level at Rio Grande City. Irregular plains as high as 1,000 feet rise at Del Rio and open hills rising to approximately 3,000 feet start at the beginnings of the Big Bend where peaks climb to 7,000 feet. In the El Paso area mountain elevations reach 4,000 feet.

Soils between the Gulf and Del Rio range from dark calcareous to neutral clays and clay loams. Dark calcareous stony clays continue with some clay loams around the Big Bend area. El Paso soil contains light reddish-brown to brown sands, calcareous clays with some salinity and rough stone lands.

Vegetation from the Gulf to Del Rio is mesquite chaparral savanna intermixed with other small trees, shrubs and cactus. The land between Del Rio and El Paso is sparsely covered with desert shrub savannah including arid-land grasses, montane forests and oak stands at higher elevations.

Mean dates of the first and last frosts in the lower valley are between November 16 and December 1 while upper valley frosts range from November 1 to November 16. The length of the warm season is different throughout the region. It varies from 320 days in the Brownsville area to 245 days around El Paso.

Mean annual precipitation in the valley varies considerably from the Gulf to the westernmost extremity. The Brownsville area has an average annual precipitation of between 24 and 28 inches, while El Paso receives as little as 8 inches per year.

The significant differences in environmental conditions create a great magnitude of variables in lifestyle, architecture and construction. Limited available materials forced builders to use earth resources like stone and adobe. Only small wood structural members are incorporated to support roofs and to construct and frame windows and doors. Much of the architecture is derived from the indigenous peoples and, later, Spanish Colonial settlers.

The earliest Spanish settlements were missions along the river in the El Paso area. They were established after a Pueblo Indian revolt in

1680 near present-day Santa Fe, New Mexico, that forced colonists to flee south.

Though the upper Rio Grande Valley between Laredo and El Paso produced the oldest architecture, the richest secular architectural resources are in the lower valley between Laredo and the Gulf. Fortunately, the missionaries, along with the Spanish overseers, thoroughly documented events, plans and statistics. Because of their dedication to accurate recording, many documents reveal information about the colo-nization of New Spain. (See, for example, Marion A. Habig, O.F.M., *Spanish Texas Pilgrimage: The Old Franciscan Missions and Other Spanish Settlements of Texas, 1632-1821* [Chicago: Franciscan Heritage Press, 1990].)

Although the lower Rio Grande Valley was settled somewhat later, it has a more diverse cultural heritage because Spain was concerned with potential French intervention in the northern frontiers. These southern and eastern regions were often referred to as the "disputed lands."

Another prominent motive for exploring and settling the region was the prospect of mineral wealth in the mountains of Tamaulipas. The crown recognized the problem of emerging hostilities from many of the Indian tribes in northern Tamaulipas, Mexico, and southern Texas and hoped that newly established settlements would act as a buffer zone between hostile forces and colonies to the south.

SAN AGUSTIN CHURCH, ORIGINALLY BUILT IN 1767

Laredo, Webb County

The Villa de San Agustín de Laredo was founded by Don Tomas Sanchez de la Barrera, a captain of the King's army, on May 15, 1755, under the auspices of Don José de Escandón, who had been charged with establishing new colonies on both sides of the Rio Grande. The planning and settlement of Laredo was one of the several villas under the supervision of Escandón. The use of the Laws of the Indies is well illustrated in the planning of the town, as evidenced by its location on the banks of the Rio Grande, San Agustín square, the location of the church, other important buildings and by the rigid grid street pattern. (For more on José de Escandón, see Sanchez, *A Shared Experience*, pp. 18-22.)

The first church was a simple jacal chapel served by friars from other missions and located on the square to the north of the present building. It was not until the early 1760s that a priest was assigned to San Agustín. It is the second oldest secular parish in Southwest United States, preceded only by San Fernando in San Antonio.

An inspection by government officials, the *Visita General*, in 1767 resulted in a specific recommendation that a proper church and convent be built on a select location on the east side of the square. There is evidence that the early church was located at a right angle to the present building and faced the Rio Grande. Parishioners were required to prepare the land

SAN AGUSTIN CHURCH *continued*

selected for the church. Each was to supply a specific number of stones weekly and to donate a portion of their time to the building of the church.

The stone church, completed in January 1789, was the first permanent religious structure in the town and has been refined, added to and continually worked on, even today. Difficult economic times, Indian raids, droughts and civil unrest discouraged the construction of a new place of worship. The original stone building was continually reworked. Finally, in 1824, foundations for a new and larger church were laid at the present site with the façade facing the square. The post-Civil War days offered some prosperity and a new church was constructed. Again, some minor modifications have taken place and the church as seen today is the product of this period.

As directed by the Laws of the Indies, the structure stands as the backdrop of the San Agustín Plaza in the oldest section

of Laredo. Although the original church was a traditional Spanish colonial mission, the edifice today is of Gothic Revival architecture. The windows and doors of the church all are surrounded by lancet arches with an oculus above the entrance and one to the left side aisle. The extended spire on the bell tower, finials at the top of the bell tower, the pilasters and the pointed arch reliefs all contribute to the strong sense of Gothic verticality. The large dentils forming the cornice at the top of the entrance façade and the upper termination of the bell tower are accented with the lancet configuration, as are the "eyebrows" over the small rectangular windows on the bell tower.

The roof is composed of two rakes on either side, accenting the center aisle and the two side aisles. Small buttresses on the side walls are symmetrically spaced between the lancet shaped windows, giving a symmetrical rhythm to the fenestration.

SAN YGNACIO RANCH BUILDINGS,

[JESUS TREVIÑO HOUSE, "THE FORT"], 1831–1871

San Ygnacio, Zapata County

In 1750 the crown authorized a land grant through colonizer Don José de Escandón to Don José Vasquez Borrego, a successful rancher from Coahuila. Borrego established his headquarters at Villa de Dolores, approximately eight miles upriver from San Ygnacio. Don Jesús Treviño, formerly of Revilla, purchased the Borrego Grant from heirs of the family and established his ranching headquarters in 1830 at a major crossing on the Rio Grande, the site that became the village of San Ygnacio.

The building erected by Treviño and later expanded by his son-in-law, Don Blas Maria Uribe, is located in the San

SAN YGNACIO RANCH BUILDINGS *continued*

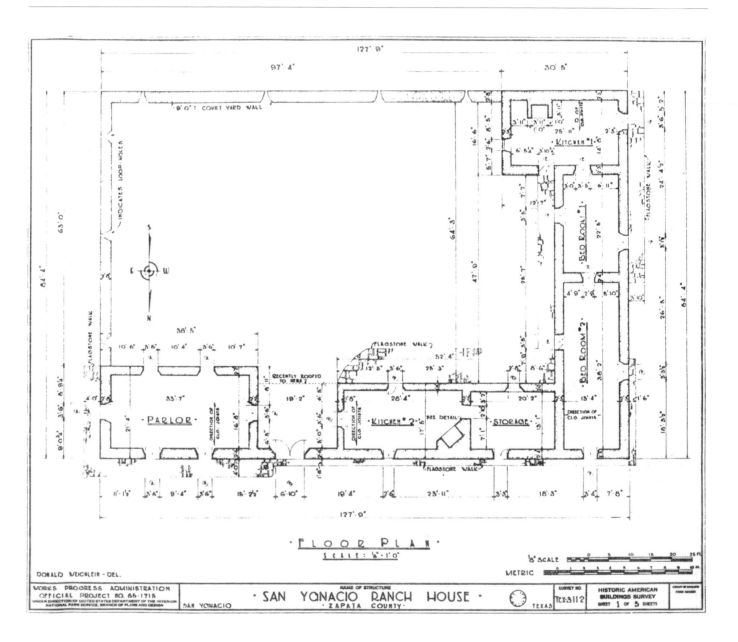

· FLOOR PLAN ·

· SAN YGNACIO RANCH HOUSE ·
· ZAPATA COUNTY ·

Ygnacio Historic District overlooking the bluffs of the Rio Grande. The primary elements are the parlor (*cella*), the entrance hall below a vaulted roof that is supported by a corbeled arched end wall with a sundial above, two kitchens (*cocinas*) with an open fireplace for cooking and chimneys extending above the roof, a storage room and two bedrooms. The oblique cant of the fireplace and chimney is unique to the second kitchen. The complex is enclosed as a courtyard or compound with stone walls closing the east and south faces, a characteristic of the Spanish/Mexican period. This arrangement creates the traditional atrium or court used for outdoor domestic functions, family privacy, security and often as a corral. The original adobe-plastered sandstone, barely obvious today, was impervious to fire and not easily penetrated by hostile Indians or other intruders.

The individual elements of the grouping are essentially homogeneous in form, materials and construction even though they were built in phases. The buildings have various roof forms: flat, vaulted and low-pitched gabled. The pitched roof over the west bedrooms and first kitchen was added at a later date and built over the original flat chipichil roof to stop water penetration through the porous lime and sand deck. The stone gargolas serve as scuppers to discharge the rainwater from the flat roof that was originally over this area.

Skilled masons using traditional cut-stone quoining to lock the corners of the intersecting walls together were responsible for the sandstone inter-locked construction.

The exterior walls range from one-foot-eight inches to two-feet-eight inches thick to offer resistance to intrusion and to provide mass to insulate from extreme temperatures. Each of the stone openings in the exterior walls appear to be doors of different dimensions, carefully beveled and fitted with wood jambs and heads. The structure has apparently never had windows.

In most designs of South Texas residences of the period, double doors allowed larger openings to maximize ventilation and cooling.

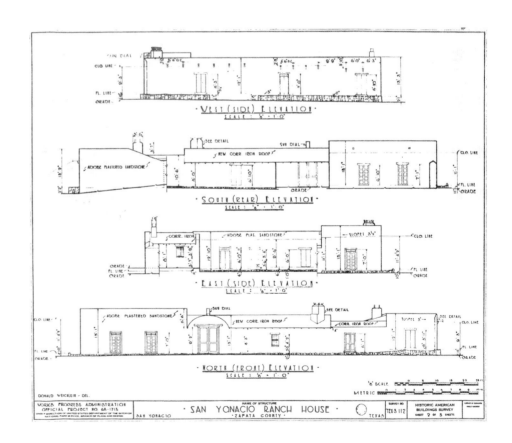

SAN RAPHAEL CHAPEL, CIRCA 1830S
Rondando, Jim Hogg County

San Raphael is a simple one-room chapel at the ranching headquarters complex at Rondando and Old Los Animas. The architectural image conforms to the Mexican/Spanish settlement period along the Rio Grande Valley. The region is relatively flat and arid and has a generous supply of native stone for construction.

The chapel is a rectangle with a gabled roof common to liturgical structures of this region and time. The bell tower is unusual, having two symmetrically spaced buttresses on either outer face that serve as the primary supporting members. The belfry itself is enclosed by a flat arch on the front and back and an oval arch opening on either of the sides. The front door gracefully fits into the niche between the two buttresses. A side door and symmetrically spaced windows offer a simple fenestration on the south wall.

The building has been well maintained although the original roof has been replaced with corrugated metal, giving a somewhat different image from the original—likely hand-split wood shakes. A salt box attachment is located on the north and to the back side of the rectangle. Construction is of stone masonry with both interior and exterior surfaces covered with white plaster. A flat ceiling covers the entire space.

MERCURIO MARTINEZ HOUSE, DATE UNKNOWN

San Ygnacio, Zapata County

The Mercurio Martinez residence is a typical nineteenth-century Spanish/Mexican structure constructed of sandstone block masonry plastered inside and out. Thick masonry walls provide mass to offer insulation during the summer months while retaining and radiating warmth during the cool evenings of winter. The white plaster coating reflects solar radiation to avoid heat build-up during the warmth of the day.

Large louvered windows and doors with transoms provide maximum ventilation while simultaneously controlling the heat and light of the summer sun. The high-hipped galvanized metal roof, likely added later above a flat chipichi roof, provides air space above to dissipate heat and shed water.

An interesting feature of this house is the attached exterior fireplace and chimney. Many San Ygnacio homes elevated the firebox approximately two feet above the floor to allow easier access for cooking. An additional fireplace opening was sometimes placed outside the house for summer cooking. The fireplace often served to heat water, warm the house during the cool months and provide for cooking and baking. The rain cover over the flue caps the step and the slope of the fireplace. The sculptural form of the fireplace and chimney, similar to several others in the community, offers a simple and sophisticated embellishment to the massing of the masonry and a visual accent to the simple rectangular cube house.

LUCAS BERGARA HOUSE, DATE UNKNOWN

San Ygnacio, Zapata County

The Lucas Bergara house, presently vacant, is constructed of sandstone. Earlier the masonry was plastered over both inside and outside. The simple rectangle has symmetrically located openings on the four walls, providing ventilation and access when opened and privacy and protection when closed. The building is erected on a shallow, slightly sloping stone podium that elevates the structure above the street and turns water away from the foundation and doorways.

The stone walls are laced together at the corners with the traditional quoining technique. Wood lintels at the head support the masonry above the openings and wood jambs frame the vertical faces. Craftsmen, pragmatic in their workmanship, used hand tools to build each of the double doors, skillfully locking the corner joints of the head, stiles and foot together with mortise and tenon joints. Double pegs through the corners secured the connection. The door panels are tongued and fitted into the prepared grooves of surrounding members, allowing the wood to expand or contract.

The skill in both the masonry construction and wood detailing reflects the high quality of craftsmanship found in Spanish/Mexican architecture of the Rio Grande Valley. Special attention was given to cutting and shaping the sandstone, laying up the heavy bearing walls, hand-cutting and planing wood to make the lintels and frames, and carefully detailing the doors.

JACAL BARN, DATE UNKNOWN
San Ygnacio, Zapata County

Most of San Ygnacio was composed of primitive jacals at one time. This building has vertical sawn timbers in the wall with horizontal wood infill. It is an excellent example of careful jacal construction, probably built during the late-nineteenth century. Considerably modified from the original, this building now has a galvanized steel roof, sawn wood board-and-batten at the gables, and corrugated steel siding on the addition in the back. This is one of the more sophisticated examples of this particular craftsmanship.

As of this writing, no documented history of the barn's dates or original functions has been found. (See William Clayton Barbee, "A Historical and Architectural Investigation of San Ygnacio, Texas," M.A. Thesis, University of Texas at Austin, 1981, and Mario L. Sanchez, *A Shared Experience: The History, Architecture and Historic Designations of the Lower Rio Grande Heritage Corridor* [Austin: Los Caminos del Rio Heritage Project and the Texas Historical Commission, 1991].)

CHARLES STILLMAN HOUSE, CIRCA 1850

Brownsville, Cameron County

The Stillman residence is an excellent example of the Greek Revival period in Texas and is one of the few found in the Rio Grande Valley. It follows traditional Spanish/Mexican Colonial design joined with Greek Revival construction. The adjoining side structure is derived from the Spanish Colonial period.

The residence is located in downtown Brownsville and was designed during the early development of the city. It is carefully scaled to the small urban site, faces the street and presents fine Greek Revival details on the front façade. Four plain columns with Doric capitals and a simple entablature at the roofline support the porch roof. The windows are symmetrically arranged around the center front door that is surrounded by glass transom and sidelights. The scale of the building and the classic details are pleasing to the eye.

The Spanish/Mexican style structure attached to the side presents a contrast to the classic revival façade. These two examples of distinct periods of architectural development, appearing side by side in a single building, suggest that the Spanish/Mexican wing was built at a different time, perhaps by another owner.

The building forms are simple rectangular cubes with generous porch roofs on the south to shade the front wall and increase ventilation for the porch. The house is constructed of brick bearing walls with white lintels above the window and door openings. The large window openings and the sheltered wall provide for minimum sun while simultaneously allowing good ventilation throughout the house.

The Spanish/Mexican style addition

NOAH COX HOUSE, CIRCA 1850

Roma, Starr County

The Noah Cox house is located off the Roma city square on a lower slope overlooking the bluffs of the Rio Grande. The original owners are thought to have been Mr. and Mrs. John Vale from Sweden, though the house is identified with Mr. Noah Cox, a later owner and prominent citizen.

The architecture of the building is unusual because of several revisions. Today it combines elements of local Spanish/Mexican culture with other unidentifiable influences. The original house, previously used for commercial purposes, had a flat roof of chipichil or tipichil. At some time prior to 1900, a hipped roof with a dormer window, not indigenous to the local Spanish/Mexican culture, was constructed over the original roof. Consequently, the build-ing presents a different image than the simple original rectangular form.

Double front doors are located on the ground floor while a single door opens to the ironwork grilled balcony. Two second-story windows flank the door symmetrically. This fenestration is altered from the original house.

The side and rear walls are constructed of local sandstone masonry and brick and covered with plaster. The plaster on the front façade is painted with white edging bands around the window and door openings, the corners, the dentil and the frieze. The side and rear corners are locked together with large quoin stones. An urban house of the 1850s, the home was built with an exterior walled courtyard.

MANUEL GUERRA RESIDENCE AND STORE, 1884

Roma, Starr County

Manuel Guerra was born in Mier, Tamaulipas, Mexico, married Noah Cox's daughter and became a prosperous merchant during the period of river and border trading. Located on the town square of the Roma Historic District, Guerra's residence and store contains the sophisticated proportioning and detailing that are unique to the design and construction skills of the master builder Heinrich Enrique Portscheller who constructed many fine structures in Starr County, including the elegant Silverio de la Peña Drugstore and post office in Rio Grande City.

Portscheller had been a European conscript into the Maximilian army and later became a fugitive after the defeat of the French-Austrian attempt to take over Mexico. Portscheller married a bride from Mier and moved his business across the Rio Grande into Texas. His classically detailed masonry buildings, built during a period of economic prosperity along the river, range from Laredo to Rio Grande City. His construction business also expanded into Mexico as far as Monterrey. Portscheller was a self-taught designer and craftsman and his efforts incorporated the classical details in buildings throughout the Rio Grande Valley. Portscheller's classical brick-masonry detailing is sophisticated, leaving a developed architecture with classical icons from the nineteenth century in the Rio Grande Valley. This was particularly true after the Civil War, when most of the architects and builders had adopted the Victorian and Italianate concepts. (See Helen Simons and Cathryn A. Hoyt, *Hispanic Texas: A Historical Guide* [Austin: University of Texas Press, 1992], pp. 253-258.)

The ground floor of the Guerra building was designed for commercial use while the second floor served as the family residence. A single-story L-shaped structure served as a warehouse and is attached to a brick wall behind the main building, forming an enclosed courtyard. The two-story portion of the building is built over a partial basement.

The fenestration of the windows and doors on the main façade provide an order and rhythm that give a strong sense of pattern. The doors and windows are articulated with classic-order details including pilasters, molded brick lintels and fascias, trademarks of Portscheller work. The cornice at the top of the façade facing the square is of molded brick with a finely scaled dentil in the shadow line. The cast iron balcony rail cantilevered from the second floor provides a horizontal organization. It once served as a family porch, perhaps derived from Portscheller's early life in Germany and Mexico. (See *The New Handbook of Texas*, vol. 5, p. 284.)

The soft buff-color brick was molded from clays dug from local soils and manufactured locally as a Portscheller product. The thick brick bearing wall construction provides excellent insulation. The large windows and doors in the second floor residence allow generous ventilation as the louvered shutters protect the interior from strong direct afternoon sunlight.

LA BORDE HOUSE, 1897

Rio Grande City, Starr County

An amalgamation of French Renaissance and Texas Victorian, the house is a sharp departure from the traditional Spanish/Mexican design concepts of this region. This building is somewhat sophisticated as a product of the French legacy of the late nineteenth century. Built later than many neighboring structures, it is an architectural landmark. During the later years of riverboat trade on the Rio Grande, it was one of the more prominent residences of the South Texas region and was the lodging place for business traders and travelers. Excellent restoration has brought it back to its original state and function as a comfortable lodging, eating and social center.

The plan is an "H" configuration with guest accommodations assigned to the two "legs," and the connecting center, or link, serving as the lobby and reception area. A well-proportioned atrium exists in the space enclosed by the guest areas on opposite sides; the link and a recent guest addition enclose the fourth side. The ingenious concept of providing each room with two exterior walls allows cross ventilation to counter the hot humid summer air. Additionally, each room has a view, privacy and protection from the sun through exterior louvered screens, a balcony and roof overhangs.

The atrium is scaled to welcome both the individual and small gatherings of people. The double galleries and their roof overhangs and the hand railings and their supporting banisters offer a sense of scale, order and architectural rhythm to the atrium and the entrance façade.

The bearing walls are of local brick with dentils below the entablatures and quoins at the corners. Parapet walls extend above the roof at the extreme ends to articulate the junctures of the masonry and the roof shingles.

WEBB-MARTINEZ HOUSE, 1897

Brownsville, Cameron County

The Webb-Martinez house is a newer building that illustrates the evolution of early Texas architecture. This is a one-story brick residence with a square plan and two unusual parallel hipped roofs set back from the masonry parapet that forms a valley between the two forms. It exhibits several Greek Revival details. The building sits on a podium that raises it several feet above the grade of the street. A covered porch on two sides shelters the walls, windows, doors and residents from the sun.

The windows—extending from floor to ceiling and covered with double shutters—are symmetrically spaced around the center doors on each façade.

Classic columns with bases and Doric capitals that are uniformly and symmetrically spaced on either side of the center entrance doors support the porch roof. (The base is not traditional on Doric capitals and columns.) The columns are slender but show sophisticated entasis. The porch fascia has classical molding and dentils that reflect the brick parapet dentils above. Sidelights and transom surround the doors.

LAS CUEVITAS, 1850–1875

Jim Hogg County

Much of Jim Hogg County was derived from a number of early Spanish land grants ranging from four to fourteen leagues. (A league represents about 2.6 square miles.) These grants were usually redistributed in smaller parcels to deserving individuals.

The town of Los Cuevitas was originally named San Antonio as early as 1805, later named San Antonio Viejo, and written on 1879 maps as Cuevitas. The site was on the first trade route from Davis Landing on the Rio Grande to the Gulf Coast region. Located at this landing, Fort Ringgold protected the traffic along the river and throughout the region. A camp for the Texas Rangers was established at the site in 1849; however, because of later changes in trade routes, the camp was moved.

Los Cuevitas is a ghost town today with the remains of what appears to be six to eight original structures and foundations. One of the buildings still standing—a simple rectangular cube with a flat roof and unembellished walls—is constructed of hand-cut caliche blocks. The interior reflects a similar simplicity. The ceiling is approximately sixteen feet high to allow hot air to rise. The deep dimension of the stone walls provided insulation from summer heat and retained interior warmth during the cold months.

Although this building is sheer and unadorned, it exhibits classic examples of masonry construction techniques derived from the Spanish/Mexican cultures. The corners are joined together with alternating interlocking stone quoins, and the flat jack arches above the door openings are constructed of tapered cut stone and locked in place by a center keystone. The weight of the stones imposed by the load of the wall creates, in addition to the download, horizontal thrust at the door and window openings which is countered by the wedge shaped stones at the jambs and allows the structural composite to maintain its configuration. Although this is a flat arch, because

LAS CUEVITAS *continued*

of the wedged stones and the horizontal thrust forces, it structurally and physically acts in the same way as a round Roman arch.

The double paneled wood doors are constructed as an upper and a lower door similar to a Dutch door. This is a practical design for hot summers and cool winter days and nights. The upper doors can be opened to allow through ventilation while the lower portion of the doors are left closed to discourage the entrance of live stock and other unwanted intrusions and keep small children inside. The hinges are details of the Spanish/Mexican period made up of two hand-forged metal interlocking eyes: one driven into the wood jamb and the other into the door stile. The wood paneled doorframe joints are secured by pegging through mortise-and-tenon joints.

The traditional Spanish/Mexican roof construction is of load-bearing wood roof joists placed in prepared niches in the walls. A layer of reeds, sticks, leaves, bark, palms or any available material, is placed over the roof joists to receive the lime and caliche three-to-four-inch poured roof deck. Because this lime caliche does not posses the high bonding qualities of modern Portland cement, water seepage eventually will lead to decomposition, requiring constant maintenance.

EUGENIO RODRIQUEZ HOUSE AND POST OFFICE, 1850 AND 1875

Las Cuevitas, Jim Hogg County

This cut limestone and plastered bearing wall construction reflects the simple technology but sophisticated craftsmanship of the late-nineteenth century in South Texas ranch country. The austerity of the Spanish/Mexican tradition is dominant in the form, the detailing of the window and door openings, the parapet at the roofline and the vernacular roof framing.

The pitched roof is not a traditional early cultural form of this region. Though this particular pitch may be original, many flat roof buildings were later modified using pitched roofs to shed rainwater more efficiently.

The roof frame is similar to modern wood construction. It is still in place less the probable wood shakes that enclosed the house and the attached porch, now collapsed. Contemporary construction incorporates horizontal wood joists to absorb the lateral thrust of pitched rafters. Because of the heavy stone walls and the light wood-framed roof, the horizontal thrust is absorbed by the wall construction so there is no need for horizontal joist members.

Eastern European Architectural Influences

A mid-nineteenth century wave of immigration brought eastern European settlers and their building styles to south-central Texas. By the early 1830s, Polish refugees from the Napoleanic Wars and the Polish Revolution began arriving in the region and were absorbed into existing communities near Galveston. But the first lasting settlement was at Panna Maria, Karnes County. Late in 1854, 100 families occupied 300 acres and, despite a winter of hardships including cold, lack of food and shelter, the majority of the community survived and flourished. Additional settlers from the Silesian area of Poland were invited to join the Texas colony, particularly those with trades and crafts in carpentry and stone masonry. During the next two decades, many Polish immigrants arrived. Much of the land in the Panna Maria area was occupied, however, so newcomers moved on to establish additional colonies. (See *The New Handbook of Texas*, vol. 5, p.254.)

CHURCH OF THE IMMACULATE CONCEPTION, 1855–1856 AND 1886

Panna Maria, Karnes County

The simple Polish settlers who came to Texas, unlike the German and French migrants, settled in the south Texas region in search of both an adequate livelihood and an escape from

oppression. Like their lifestyle in the mother country, the settlers sought a simple agrarian way.

Father Leopold Moczygemba brought 100 colonists to this remote region to build their new lives and homes. Their first winter was dreadfully uncomfortable, made so by heavy rains, wind and sub-freezing weather. As the colony became established and prospered through the long summer, they constructed their first permanent structure, the Church of Immaculate Conception in 1855 and 1856. It is the oldest Polish parish in the nation. In 1877, due to deterioration of the mortar of the original structure, the present church was rebuilt and remains the same today.

The white plastered building is situated on a prominent elevation and is highly visible from the surrounding landscape. The simple form of this building, with the prominent bell tower and steep roof, accents its visibility. The arched lancet windows offer a subtle Gothic adornment to the fenestration of the façades. The buttresses countering the outward thrust created on the side walls articulate wall segments and window spacing.

The bell tower is stepped with a subtle reduction of the form at each level, giving a sense of greater verticality, and is accented by the steep spire above. The fenestration of the double front door and the lancet arched louvered openings emphasize the verticality.

JOHN GAWLIK HOUSE, 1858

Panna Maria, Karnes County

John Gawlik, an accomplished stone mason and the builder and owner of this first stone house in the Panna Maria community, arrived in Texas in 1855. Gawlik participated in the construction of the Church of the Immaculate Conception and most likely assisted in constructing homes for other settlers.

The house is configured as a near-square plan covered by an asymmetric, steeply pitched gabled roof with a large overhang

covering the front porch. The first floor contains a large room across the width of the front of the house and a narrow room to the back. The front room is floored with wood planks; the back room and the porch have stone floors. A wood-floored loft is located directly under the gabled roof with original access by ladder through a door in the gable. The exterior stone walls are approximately two feet thick with a door at the center and two symmetrically placed windows flanking the door on the front and back elevations. Two small square windows in the west gable and a door in the opposite gable allow cross ventilation through the loft.

Four octagonal shaped columns and a chimney that extended above the roof from the inside west wall fireplace originally supported the porch roof overhang. Wood shakes originally covered the roof and the stone walls were plastered. The house is preserved and now serves as a hay barn.

The simple forms and details of this dwelling are unique to the Upper Silesian rural houses. Other Panna Maria buildings include similar configurations and details.

JOHN KOWALIK HOUSE, CIRCA 1860

Panna Maria, Karnes County

Records do not indicate the exact date the John Kowalik house was built; however, local opinion suggests that it was likely constructed about 1860. It is a classic example of an Upper Silesian agrarian residence.

The simple rectangular cube with a gabled roof is designed to provide shelter from seasonal weather changes. The generous porch and slightly flatter roof rake offer an interesting visual image while providing protection from the weather. When siting a house, intelligent pioneers usually placed the front exposure to the south to allow the low winter sun to penetrate below the porch overhang and give light and warmth to the wall, windows and door openings. During warm months while

JOHN KOWALIK HOUSE *continued*

the sun is high in the sky, the porch roof shades these surfaces. In addition, the front exposure provides a splendid view overlooking the San Antonio River valley. The southwest breezes have a cooling effect in the summer while the back walls deflect the northwest winter winds. The east and west walls are small and receive less exposure to the summer sun during late morning and afternoon.

The house has three rooms on the first floor with the largest enclosed by heavy stone walls. A smaller rectangular room extends from the west end of the stone wall, and a long rectangular room is attached to the back of the house. Both of the smaller rooms are roofed in wood and floored with wood planking. A gabled roof covers the side room, while a slightly flatter rake similar to the porch cover shelters the back room,

giving the house symmetry. The entire roof was originally covered with wood shakes. Five asymmetrically spaced hexagonal shaped wood columns support the porch roof. The stonework is well crafted using hand-chiseled faced stone with carefully fitted joints quoined at the corners. White plaster originally covered the walls inside and out, however the exterior plaster has eroded and broken away, totally exposing the stone work.

The west wall masonry includes two back-to-back fireplaces that face into the east and west rooms and feed into a single chimney. The loft is directly under the gabled roof with one opening on the east elevation directly above the window below.

The simple form and economic construction and detail offer a fundamental elegance that typifies the time, location and ethnic culture to which the house belongs.

IMMACULATE CONCEPTION CATHEDRAL, 1856–1859

Brownsville, Cameron County

Immaculate Conception Cathedral, a Gothic Revival structure of mid-century architecture, was designed by the French-trained architect and priest Father Pierre Yves Kéralum. This edifice is one of the most sophisticated of the liturgical buildings of nineteenth-century Texas design.

In 1849, Bishop J. M. Odin of Galveston determined that a cathedral should be built in Brownsville, the first permanent settlement of the Oblate Fathers of Mary Immaculate in the United States. In March of 1850 land was purchased and a plan for a chapel was drafted after using a barn for the priests' quarters and holding mass in an abandoned commercial building. The small chapel was completed in June of the same year. Plans were then developed for a larger permanent chapel and, on July 6, 1856, construction began. The church was finished on June 12, 1859. Bishop Odin offered the blessing and dedicated the church to the Immaculate Conception. After a century of liturgical and physical changes, the edifice was designated a cathedral and, a decade later, the seat of the Diocese of Brownsville.

The primary entrance to the Latin cross plan is on the north façade. The structure has evenly spaced brick buttresses supported by the brick foundation walls that counter the thrust placed on the outer walls, then rise vertically to forty feet. The side wall parapets extend slightly above the roof eave line. The present asbestos shingle roof maintains a twelve-in-twelve rake gabled roof some seventy feet above grade to the ridge.

A square brick tower accents the entrance and rises eighty-eight feet. It features a heavily molded brick and wood recessed lancet-arch entrance. Above the portal is a large stained glass lancet-arch window, flanked by two smaller similar windows.

The interior ceiling is ribbed, vaulted and paneled with painted canvas, often used in the Gothic churches in South

IMMACULATE CONCEPTION CATHEDRAL *continued*

Texas. The interior roof supports are composed of eight pleasing, uniformly spaced clustered piers, plastered and painted and attached to the nave walls. The nave floor of green terrazzo provides contrast to the rich red carpet that covers the chancel and the apse.

The original wood altar was ornately carved and trimmed in gold leaf. In 1960, the Second Vatican Council required that the original altar, attached to the apse, be moved forward on the chancel and replaced with an unadorned marble table. An unembellished podium replaced the original Kéralum pulpit.

The Madonna Chapel, surmounted by a high grill and the coat of arms of Mariano S. Garriga (Bishop of Corpus Christi), is an appendage from the exterior of the nave. Successive restorations have assured the preservation of the cathedral. In 1963 an exterior restoration and re-roofing were completed and in 1965 the interior was restored, bringing back the original beauties of the nave by replacing and painting the canvas ceiling, walls and columns. In 1970, after a damaging fire, further restoration to stabilize the intrusion of rising moisture in the masonry walls was undertaken.

IMMACULATE CONCEPTION CATHEDRAL *continued*

LA LOMITA CHAPEL, 1865
Mission, Hidalgo County

This chapel was built by the Oblate Fathers of Mary Immaculate, at the place of rendezvous of the "Padres on Horseback," in transit between Roma and Brownsville. The site is on a 122-acre ranch of the original Oblate Fathers. The building is a simple rectangular plan and open ceiling following the configuration of the gabled roof. The plastered stone masonry bearing walls and the shingled roof are representative of the architecture of the Spanish/Mexican period. This basic building design and construction provide insulation from solar radiation and the generous window and door openings allow good cross ventilation.

The parapets at the two end walls extend above the roof line, articulating the contrast of the white of the walls against the darker value of the wood shingle roof. The accent of the juncture of the two planes and the different construction technologies of the two materials present a visual contrast of light and dark. The petit belfry, an appendage to the roof, emphasizes the delicate scale of the chapel and its details.

AMADOR VELA STORE, CIRCA 1870S
San Ygnacio, Zapata County

The Amador Vela store faces the central square of the San Ygnacio National Historic District. The pristine form of the flat-roofed building is an excellent example of unaltered architecture from the Mexican/Spanish period. The original simple rectangular solid was added to about the turn of the century by enclosing a room at the back and adding a porch to the east side and the rear wall.

The fenestration of the front façade is asymmetrical around a centered plaster pilaster, the doors and windows symmetrically located on either side of the center line. The continuous metal fascia, the large plaster dentils immediately below, the soffit, and the plaster molding, provide an order which visually ties the long façade together. The plaster pseudo quoins at the corners serve as ornaments.

The building is constructed of native sandstone and is covered with white lime plaster on both the exterior and interior. The masonry is of cut stone, laid in horizontal bond, obviously by a skilled mason. The floors are wood and beaded-wood planking on the ceiling completes the design.

The wooden door and window frames were set in place prior to the masonry construction; hence each stone fits to the wood; plaster covers the joints. Two doors appear to be constructed of a series of vertical boards and the door facing the square has four panels. Each has a transom light above.

RANCHO DE SANTA MARIA, 1870

Hidalgo County

Rancho de Santa Maria, built by L. J. Haynes in 1870, is a two-story masonry structure typical of the Spanish/Mexican architecture of the period. The building has served as a ranching headquarters as well as a fort. The complex is composed of a primary house, two tenant residences, agricultural storage and processing structures, an armory, a bath house and various water storage and irrigation systems. Although the forms which make up the composite are simple, the relationships of the various parts becomes complex as a group.

The visual and functional aims of these buildings have been considerably changed since the original construction because of hurricane damage and remodeling to accommodate present uses. The changes of construction, materials and details suggests that revisions have been significant. The simple forms of the individual elements—unique to the region and period—are enriched by the details. On the east façade, the windows are symmetrically located on either side of the major door and the arcaded porch provides shelter from southern exposure. The brick detailing at the cornice of the residence and the outbuildings offers relief to the austere masonry walls.

The complex, which now sits in agricultural fields, was once located adjacent to the Rio Grande and has now been isolated as a result of changes in the course of the river.

Rancho de Santa Maria is significant both visually and functionally. Architecturally, the complex shows a variety of forms that utilize local brickwork details. Historically, the complex was associated with early farming interests and was in concert with military sites along the border, specifically between Fort Brown and Fort Ringgold.

Nativity of the Blessed Virgin Mary Church, 1878

Czestochowa, Karnes County

This church was established by forty families in 1874 as a result of their separation from the original 1854 Polish settlement at Panna Maria. It is located approximately five miles to the southwest of the village of Czestochowa. The structure was built in 1878 of local limestone and plastered over on the exterior and interior. The crucifix plan is composed of a narthex immediately behind the front doors, a nave and an intersecting transept with the apse at the farmost end. The form of the church is derived from the Gothic Revival, using finial capped buttresses supporting the walls and delineating the five bays housing the nave.

The massing, although made of many parts including the bell tower, the narthex, nave, transept and apse, is of simple forms masterfully composed into the complex. The assemblage emphasizes the vertical. The lancet arched windows, pediment and niche over the entrance doors, the pointed arch relief below the roof line, the steeply pitched roof, the finials on the bell tower and above the buttresses and the steep copper spire at the top of the bell tower accentuate this spirit.

POST CHAPEL, DATE UNKNOWN

Fort McIntosh, Laredo, Webb County

The early buildings in most frontier military posts, including those in Texas, were crude temporary structures erected to house soldiers and their ordnance until the fort was authorized as a permanent facility. After permanent status was granted, posts received the financial support to construct more durable buildings, usually under contracts negotiated with civilians. Fort McIntosh—established in 1849 and named for Lieutenant Colonel James S. McIntosh who was killed in the battle of Molino del Rey in the Mexican-American War—was deactivated on June 9, 1947.

The chapel is an example of Classic Revival architecture with detailing exhibited in the portico of the front façade. This classic treatment suggests an influence from the traditional Palladian design. The pediment, surrounded by a classic molding, is supported by a thin entablature and in turn is carried by four pairs of columns rising from brick pedestals.

The double front door is surrounded by glass side lights and above by a half-round fan light with a keystone at the peak of the round brick masonry arch. The windows are symmetrically placed on either side of the entrance, the upper windows have a shallow brick arch above for masonry support and the lower have heavy lintels above.

The chapel now houses the book stores for Laredo Junior College and Texas A & M International.

THE OLD CONVENT [PARISH HALL], 1880

Roma, Starr County

The Old Convent, adjacent to Our Lady of Refuge Bell Tower, overlooks the bluffs of the town square in the Roma Historical District. Roma—one of the colonias on the north side of the Rio Grande—dates to the 1760s. It was established by Don José de Escandón's colonization efforts. Because this was the last navigable point on the river and because it was a major crossing spot on the trail from Mier, Tamaulipas, to the Gulf Coast of Texas, much legal trade and contraband passed through Roma. Such wealth passing through the community during its greatest period of prosperity, made available the resources to construct elegant homes, commercial structures and other buildings.

The convent, the only such institution between Laredo and Brownsville, is one of the significant brick structures designed and built by master builder Heinrich Enrique Portscheller. Portscheller, who contributed a richness to the valley region

through his classic revival designs and construction, trained local craftsmen in the design of brick masonry.

The original function of the building was to provide quarters for the Sisters of the Incarnate Word and later the Sisters of Mercy, who offered instruction to the young girls of Roma.

The form of the building is longitudinal, one-story with bayed ends, a high-pitched roof with a wood cupola, a covered porch across the main façade and exquisite brick details articulating the entrances.

The convent exhibits Portscheller's talents in the brick detailing of the pilasters and pediment at the doors. His abilities to mold brick and to set the units in mortar illustrate his sensitivity to design as well as his sophisticated skill in masonry technology.

Portscheller's design, framing the end door of the convent, is of particular interest, since it illustrates his use of classic detail. The door opening is framed by brick pilasters on either side with a molded base and capital. A plain entablature of brick, laid as a jack arch, rests on the pilaster capitals. The pediment is likewise composed of molded brick, laid to form the flat triangular form, with tiny molded brick dentils underneath. The entrance and the wall at the bays are well detailed, giving refined scale to the façade.

TOLUCA RANCH: STORE, SCHOOL AND ST. JOSEPH'S CHURCH

Hidalgo County

The Toluca Ranch—10,000 acres of the fertile valley ground bordering on the Rio Grande—was a grant acquired by Juan José Hinojosa and later sold to Florencio Sáens in 1880. It has been, and continues to be, one of the few self-sustaining ranches of this region. The land has not only provided for the maintenance and development of the property but has also furnished the building materials and maintenance for all the structures on the property. The bricks were hand formed and fired from available clay and laid by local masons for the school, store, residence and church.

The school and the store are composed as one single "L"-shaped plan, both constructed in 1908; both are indigenous to Mexican concepts of architecture. The school was one of the first public schools built in Hidalgo County. The brick arcade on the river side of the edifice provides support for the gently sloping roof, gives shade to the exterior wall immediately behind and presents an architectural rhythm to this façade. The interior walls also follow the same arched trace and provide structural support for the flat roof.

The brick coping, covering the parapet of the store and school, is laid up as a sailor course to shed rain from the core of the thick brick walls. In order to protect the exterior walls, the coping extends approximately two inches beyond the masonry wall and works to discharge rain water beyond the outside wall surfaces. The coping follows graceful curves atop the parapets—an ingenious technique that approximates the rake of the roof and offers a graceful and unique facade. The tallest wall is embellished with corbeled brick molding and brick dentils. The door and window heads are all supported by shallow brick arches.

The residence is a composite of Mexican/Victorian design and is situated between the store and school and St. Joseph's Church.

The church has been in continual use since its construction in 1889 and is used as a private chapel of the Sáenz family and ranch workers. The French priest-architect, Father Pierre Kéralum, O.M.I., designed and oversaw the building of the Gothic Revival St. Joseph's Church. Construction was supported by the family in thanksgiving to God for the discovery of good potable water nearby. Father Kéralum also built churches in Brownsville, Roma, Santa Maria, Rio Grande City and Laredo.

The church plan is the traditional cruciform configuration, the bell tower being the tall rectangular form capped by a tall thin spire and centered on the front facade. The narthex, enclosed by the lower walls of the bell tower, marks the primary entrance, an opening through double doors within a lancet aperture with a pointed fan window. From the narthex, one

TOLUCA RANCH: STORE, SCHOOL AND ST. JOSEPH'S CHURCH *continued*

enters into a single aisle nave. At the end of the pews and aisle is a single small step up to the chancel, then beyond to the apse, the alter and retablo. Two rooms on either side of the chancel, isolated by walls and doors, appear from the exterior to be the transept; however, in reality they serve as vesting areas or for other secondary functions.

The stepped buttresses and the lancet windows on the side walls are characteristic of the Gothic Revival style. St. Joseph's Church has heavy brick walls. Roof framing is constructed from trussed wood timbers. Accordingly, very little horizontal thrust exists, suggesting the purpose of the buttresses gives only stabilization to the vertical loading of the side walls and accents the symmetrical visual spacing order between the windows.

Two delicately corbeled brick moldings and detailed brick dentils on the bell tower are carried onto the masonry parapet on the front façade and at the gables of the two side rooms. Finials project above the three stepped buttresses and a small star is mounted on each of the two front corners. A small metal star appears on each of the corner buttresses.

OUR LADY OF VISITATION, 1882

Hidalgo County

This Gothic Revival church was built by the Oblate Fathers as one of their valley missions between Brownsville and Roma. The building is unique to this region and is a product of French priest Father Pierre Kéralum.

The simple massing, derived from the cruciform plan, traditional throughout most of the Gothic architecture, offers proportions suggesting an emphasis on the vertical. Originally, a wood spire, lost to the winds of a storm, provided a greater prominence to the vertical emphasis.

The light brown colored brick was made from the local clays at nearby Rancho de Santa Maria. The masonry is skillfully worked into the development of the Gothic details includ-

OUR LADY OF VISITATION *continued*

ing the lancet eyebrows above the windows and the entrance doors, the finials above the parapet walls at each corner of the building and bell tower and the pointed dentils at the frieze of the bell tower. The stepped buttresses at the corners, symmetrically and rhythmically punctuated by the windows on the side walls, offer an order to the design. The brick dentils, the frieze, the panels in the doors and the grid of the muttons and mullions of the windows, offer a rapport with the human scale.

Although the form suggests a transept, this space—likely used for vesting—is separated from the chancel and the nave by masonry walls. Access is offered through doors to the chancel and through a second set of doors leading to the exterior.

NESTER SEAN'S STORE, 1884

Roma, Starr County

This commercial structure is located just outside the city square and backs up to the bluffs overlooking the Rio Grande. The brick masonry bearing construction and classic details are clear Heinrich Portscheller trademarks. The four bay, flat roof, single-story "L- shaped" plan is elegantly simple. The scale is finely articulated by the classic brick moldings, pilasters, entablatures, dentils around the openings, corners and the fascia. The double doors of cypress, although in poor repair, are gracefully paneled with a grilled transom above for ventilation and light.

Although this building has been allowed to deteriorate through neglect, vandalism and fire, it still retains the dignity of a classic Portscheller design.

HIDALGO COUNTY POST OFFICE, 1886
Hidalgo, Hidalgo County

The old Hidalgo County Post Office is one of three buildings built as a civic complex during the 1880s. In addition to this structure, there is a courthouse and a jail. After the county seat was moved to Edinburg, the three buildings were adapted as low income residences and, at times, abandoned and allowed to deteriorate. This building is of the late Spanish/Mexican period of settlement of the Rio Grande Valley.

The pristine simplicity of the solid rectangular form and the ordered rhythm of the openings in the façade give this building an unadorned elegance. The ability to open the numerous doors and windows of the edifice allows for optimal air movement and cooling during the warm months. The massive brick masonry walls absorb heat during the day and inversely radiate warmth during the cooler hours of the evening.

The richly ornamented brick detailing at the frieze is unusual. The masonry dentil detailing with the corbeled coursing above enriches the visual image of the cornice, a unique vignette of the valley of the late nineteenth century. This garnishing may have been influenced by Heinrich Portscheller's masonry detailing.

The wood lintels above the doors and windows are visually and structurally interesting. The diagonal shaping of the lintel ends and the canted masonry seating offers a locking technique, securing the materials into a homogeneous structure and supporting the heavy masonry above the door and window heads.

SILVERIO DE LA PENA DRUGSTORE AND POST OFFICE, 1886

Rio Grande City, Starr County

The Silverio de la Peña Drugstore, post office and residence was designed and built by Heinrich Portscheller. The business of the Silverio de la Peña Drugstore and post office was conducted from the street floor; the second floor was assigned as residential quarters. The subtle brown bricks, manufactured and fired in Portscheller's brickyard, bonded together with the similar value mortar, offer a limited palette of color. The simple form of this two-story rectangular cube is well scaled and proportioned to the surrounding edifices of Rio Grande City.

Although the form of the building is simple, it is a substantial departure from the traditional Spanish/Mexican architecture of the region. The Classic Revival masonry detailing is unique to Portscheller's work. The fluted pilasters with Doric capitals articulate the corners of the building with round Roman arches rising from pronounced spring stones at the doors accenting the entrances. The classic entablature, consisting of the architrave with uniform separations of sets of five dentils each, the frieze with a low relief of masonry medallions spaced in concert with the dentils of the architrave and finally the crowning cornice with a molded masonry soffit and a continuous band of dentils, are supported by the same brick-colored bearing walls.

ROMA MUSEUM, DATE UNKNOWN

Roma, Starr County

This structure was built to house the First Catholic Church. It was later converted to the Roma Museum. The architecture is typical of nineteenth-century Spanish/Mexican influence in the Rio Grande settlements. The form is an "L" configuration with a large open room, originally the nave, and an adjoining wing with smaller rooms that likely served as the sacristy. The gabled, high-pitched roof over the large room creates a tall open perception in the primary room. The "L" configuration creates two sides of a walled courtyard. The two simple rectangular forms of different heights with gabled roofs intersect as a common wall, contributing to the restrained massing of the edifice.

The design allows for climate modification, using the heavy bearing stone plastered walls as mass to insulate from the heat and solar gain during the summer months and providing enclosure to confine warmth during the cool months. The high gabled ceilings allow warm air to rise above the level of occupation, while the generous window and door openings provide for cross ventilation.

Glossary

acequia—A canal, trench or drain.

adobe—A sun-dried water clay mud matrix hand molded into a rectangular solid brick configuration, approximately 38 cm. by 38 cm. by 8 cm. in dimension.

adz (or adze)—A cutting tool used to shape logs with an arching blade at right angles to the handle.

apse—Semicircular or polygonal termination space of a church adjoining the chancel at the most eastern position of the traditional crucifix plan. It is usually the location of the altar.

arcade—A continuous series of supporting arches.

arch—A curved structure formed of wedge-shaped blocks of brick or stone (voussoirs) held together by mutual pressure and supported on the sides. Semicircular arch: a semicircle having its center on the springing line. Stilted arch: an arch sprung from a point above the imposts. The vertical masonry between the imposts and springing line resembles stilts. Horseshoe arch: a stilted arch with the masonry between the springing line and imposts, including inwards. Elliptical arch: a half-ellipse drawn from a center below the springing line. Trefoil arch: a rounded or pointed arch springing from the apex of two separated rounded arches. Pointed arch: a compound of two arcs drawn from centers on the springing line. Lancet arch: a narrow pointed arch whose span is shorter than the radii. Equilateral arch: an arch whose span is equal to the radii. Drop arch: an arch whose span is greater than the radii. Three-centered arch: two separated arches with centers on springing line, surmounted by a segmental arch with center below springing line. Four-centered Tudor arch: a depressed pointed arch composed of two pairs of arches, the lower pair drawn from two centers on the springing line and the upper pair from centers below the springing line. Ogee arch: a pointed arch formed of two convex arcs above and two concave arcs below. Shouldered arch: having shoulders, i.e. with projecting stones resting on the horizontal course, sometimes called Caernarvon arch.

architrave—The lowest of the main divisions of an entablature. Also, the molded frame surrounding a door or window.

ashlar—Square hewn stone laid in regular courses with fine joints.

attic or loft—A room situated within the roof of a building. Also, the upper story above the main cornice.

audencia—Audience, a hearing given by men in power to those who have something to propose or present.

balcony—A platform projecting from an exterior or interior wall of a building above ground level, enclosed by a railing or balustrade and supported frequently by wood or iron brackets.

baluster—Any of a number of closely spaced supports for a railing.

balustrade—A series of balusters supporting a rail or coping.

baptistry—A place or enclosed space where the rite of baptisms are administered.

barge board—A corruption of verge board. These boards are placed on the verge of a gable to screen the projecting roof timbers and to prevent the penetration of rainwater.

baroque—A term principally applied to Renaissance architecture, painting, and sculpture beginning in Italy in the early 17th century, and primarily in Rome in the seventh century. Its architecture is characterized by dynamic spatial effects, often achieved by the integration of painting and sculpture, and deliberately aimed at involving the spectator physically as well as emotionally. Spanish baroque was introduced in the New World after the death of Philip II and became a prominent architecture in the liturgical structures. (See Harris and Lever, *Illustrated Glossary* . . . .)

barrel vault—an arched roof or ceiling of semicircular section.

bastion—a projection from the outer wall of a fortification.

beam—A wood, steel, stone, or concrete horizontal or diagonal member used to maintain the configuration of a building while carrying live and/or dead loads.

belfry—That part of a tower or steeple in which a bell or bells are hung.

board and batten—Vertical wood bearing wall construction assembled by boards nailed to a sill plate and a head. Joints are covered with smaller boards or strips to close the wall from the elements.

brickwork—Header course: bricks are laid so that the head ends of the brick are exposed. Flemish bond: consists of coursing bricks laid so that the header and stretcher alternate in the wall. stretcher bond: laid so that only the side or the stretcher shows in the wall face. English bond: consists of alternating courses of stretcher and headers. Virginia running bond: stretcher coursing with continuous headers at each sixth course. Gauged brickwork: brick wall laid with very fine joints.

buttress—A mass of brick or stone built against a wall to provide lateral stability.

cabin—A small, often crudely built dwelling or outbuilding often consisting of unshaped or, on occasion, shaped logs.

caliche—A traditional material of the region composed of pebble or small pieces of limestone accidentally introduced into brick or tile at the time of its being burned. Also, it may be a crust of lime that flakes from a wall (also see chipichil).

canales—Scuppers or projected spouts attached to the roof to discharge rainwater away from the building walls or foundation.

canopy—A projected cover or roof over a specific element of the architecture.

cantilever—A structural member projecting beyond the supporting member.

capital—The uppermost part of a column or pilaster usually ornamented by one of the five classic orders.

carrizo—Reeds or similar cane matting often woven into a curtain or mat.

cat or mud cat—A chimney built of mud, usually combined with moss, grass, straw, or horsehair as a binding agent, enclosed by rough cut wood member framing uniformly stacked horizontally on four sides. These chimneys were often constructed as a leaning tower, supported by a single wood pole to counter gravitational collapse.

cedela—A strip of parchment or paper to be written upon; an order, bill, decree, or warrant.

cella—A parlor or living room.

chancel—The space in a church between the nave and the apse, usually slightly elevated, providing for the lectern and the pulpit.

chink—A roughly shaped, solid-form parallelogram, usually cut and split with an ax, used for infill between logs in a wall construction.

chinking—Placing parallelogram shaped pieces of rough-cut wood (chink) between the logs of a log construction, then driving horizontally with the longitudinal plane of the wall, then plastering over with mud, lime cement or, in modern restorations, Portland cement mortar. Rocks, sod, mud or other easily available materials may be used as the chinking.

chipichil or tipichil—A local term for lime concrete containing finely crushed limestone pea gravel aggregate that is used in roofing, paving, or flooring. In roofing, beams, or vigas, are placed in prepared niches in masonry walls, and covered over with small pieces of wood (latias), palm leaves, reeds or the available local materials. This construction serves as form work to receive the lime concrete poured roof. Its primary advantage is that it insulates from the sun's heat during the warm months and retains the inside warmth during the cool periods. The primary disadvantage of this material is water penetration, which causes decomposition and leakage over a period of time. Consequently many of the early Spanish/Mexican buildings have had hipped and pitched roofs composed of water repellent materials built over the flat roof, thereby, changing the configuration of the entire building.

colonia—Colony, plantation, subdivision of a city, or residential districts.

colonnade—A continuous series of vertical supports, usually in the form of columns.

column—A vertical supporting member. In classical architecture, it consists of a base, shaft, necking and capital.

Composite order (or Roman)—A column that combines the predominant volutes of the Ionic and the acanthus of the Corinthian on its capital and is thus the most decorative. The shaft may be fluted or plain.

convento—Convent of monks, friars, or nuns; monastery, nunnery; a community of religious men or women.

Corinthian order—A bell-shaped capital from which eight acanthus stalks (caulicoli) emerge to support the modest volutes.

cornice—The uppermost member of an entablature. Also, any molded projection which crowns or finishes the part to which it is fixed, e.g., a wall, door, or window.

crenulate—In botany, having a notched, indented, or scalloped edge.

crib—A log enclosure usually composed of a single rectangular cube, often identified as a log outbuilding.

crossett—Any of the small projecting pieces in a stone or wood arch that hang upon the adjacent members; also the return on the corners of the door cases or window frames; also called an ear, elbow, ancon.

cylinder—a solid circular form having continuous equal diameter.

cyucks—stone or wood member or bracket usually attached to a wall often used to support the ridge beam.

dentil—One of a series of small rectangular blocks arranged like a row of teeth projecting from the lower part of the Ionic, Corinthian, Composite and sometimes, Doric cornices.

dog run or dog trot—A two-crib log house in an "I" configuration, placed with parallel gables, of one or two stories separated by an open roofed

space used as a breezeway during warm weather. It is sometimes enclosed during cool weather or occasionally to provide an additional room.

dome—A convex covering, usually hemispherical or semi-elliptical, over a circular or polygonal space.

Doric order—The column has no base. The capital is plain; the shaft is fluted.

draw knife—A single slightly curved steel blade having a "pull" type handle at either end, primarily used for smoothing and tapering roof shakes or shingles.

dugout—A structure usually built completely into the earth.

eared Gothic molding—A molding, having ear-like parts or appendages.

Eastlake—A substyle of the Folk Victorian commonly emphasizing turned spindles.

entablature—In the classical orders, the assembly of horizontal members, architrave, frieze and cornice, supported by a column. These members may also be on a wall without columnar support.

entices—A very light convex curve or swelling on the profile of a column shaft intended to counteract the optical illusion of concavity. It occurs most frequently in classical architecture, especially Greek. In America, it is found in the Greek Revival examples.

espadaña—Reed-mace, great cat-tail, typha latifolia, spire. A biological term used in describing certain elements of Spanish architecture.

façade—The face or front of a building but especially the principal front.

fachwerk—A traditional framing construction used in vernacular German buildings composed of a post and beam construction with diagonal brac-

ing within the frame to counter lateral forces. Such framing was filled with stone, brick and adobe.

fascia—A long flat member or band, e.g., the horizontal division of an architrave; the flat board covering the ends of rafters under the eaves; or the name board over a shop window.

fenestration—The arrangement of windows in a wall, usually having some pattern to accommodate light emission, ventilation, visual exposure and aesthetic attraction.

finial—a small ornament (or decorative knob) at the top or at the sides of a gable.

flutes, fluting—The vertical grooves on the shaft of a column, pilaster or other surface of semicircular, segmental or semi-elliptical section. The flutes may meet in an arris or be separated by a fillet. Also called striges.

Folk Victorian (1870-1910)—Identifying characteristics include porches with spindlework detailing or flat, jigsaw cut trim, a symmetrical façade, and cornice-line brackets.

frieze—The part of an entablature between the architrave and the cornice; or any similar decorative band of feature.

froe—An iron "L"-shaped blade with wood handle attached at a right angle; used in the preparation of boards, puncheons, shakes, and shingles.

full-dovetail notch—A type of log corner notching formed by cutting diagonal faces at the inside of the wall. This joint, though attractive and a secure lock, does not shed water on the lower member, thus causing decay and gradual joint disintegration.

fusiform—A spindle, shaped like a spindle; thick, tapered at each end.

gable—The triangular portion of a wall at the end of a ridge roof.

gallery—Sometimes referred to as a veranda; a front porch, frequently upper level on a two-story house, usually on the front façade used for protecting the wall from sun and rain and providing an exterior space for casual living.

gargola—Members at the end or at the side edge of a gutter or roof dam for the purpose of discharging water as a stream; similar to a scupper or an unadorned gargoyle.

gingerbread—The wood detail used primarily in the Victorian style to ornament columns, banisters, galleries, the roof soffit below the gables. Gingerbread was a product of the Industrial Revolution, which allowed fanciful ornamentation to be turned or cut by a lathe or a jig saw.

Gothic—The style of architecture succeeding the Norman or Romanesque and subdivided chronologically and stylistically into several periods. It may be generally characterized by the use of the pointed arch and the vault.

Gothic Revival—The recreation of the form, mass and the decoration and concepts of Gothic architecture.

Greek Revival—The recreation of the form, mass, and decoration using traditional Greek architecture as the pattern or model.

groined vault or cross vault—Vaulting that is formed by the intersection of two barrel vaults at right angles from the arched diagonals or groins.

gutjae or guttae—Small "drops" or conic projections under the mutules and triglyphs of a Doric entablature.

half-dovetail notch—A corner notching formed by cutting the top side of the end of the log sloping down toward the outside of the joint, leaving the remaining portion on the inside of the wall. This notch has greater advantage over the full dovetail notch in that it sheds water by gravity.

half dugout—A primitive homestead in which the walls are built half into the earth.

high renaissance—A liturgical architectural style of great simplicity established by Spain in the New World. It uses the basic elements of the classical period on stern dictates of Philip II.

huilotes—Smaller frequently 3-by-4-inch wood members similar to a subpurlin laid usually over and perpendicular to the latias or purlins.

icon—An image, a figure, a representation, a likeness, a semblance to represent a particular period or ornament in architecture.

Ionic order—Lighter, more elegant than the Doric, with slim columns, generally fluted. It is principally distinguished by the volutes of its capital.

jacal—Palasado, thatch, stone or sometimes mud huts for domestic storage or animal shelter.

jack arch—A flat masonry arch frequently above windows and doors acting with similar horizontal thrust as the traditional arch, countered by walls and a key stone.

jamb—The vertical side member of a door or a window, or of the door or window frame.

junta—A congress, an assembly, a council, a convention, a tribunal.

keystone—A central wedge-shaped block or voussoir, placed as the apex center stone of an arch, in which gravity of the load locks the whole together. Sometimes ornamented with embellishments such as sculpted carvings.

lancet (referred to as a lancet arch or Gothic arch)—A tall narrow pointed window, sometimes door opening, characteristic of early English architecture, often grouped in threes, fives or sevens at the east end of a church.

lantern—A small circular or polygonal structure raised on a dome or roof in order to admit light. Also, applied to that stage of a central tower of a church, containing windows to light the crossing.

latias—Small pieces of wood resting on the vigas, often placed with diagonal configuration, to serve as roof covering.

lattice—A bower, a cover, an open shelter, a trellis, an arbor, frequently used to embellish or to provide shade and protection from the sun and solar buildup.

log cabin—A one-room structure used for a dwelling or an outbuilding.

log house—A house of two or more rooms often with an upper floor or garret, usually of carefully shaped logs and joints.

mallet—An impacting tool with a hammer configuration usually composed of a hard wood head and handle.

mass—An accumulation of forms to create a more complex form.

metope—The space between Doric triglyphs.

miter—Used in joinery, the shaping of two moldings, trim, brick, or stones, the joining faces cut at 45 degree angles, allowing the members to fit together forming a right-angle joint.

molding—A plain or enriched band used as an ornamental decoration or to protect a wall or other surface. Each style of architecture produces its own characteristic section configuration.

mortar and rubble—In masonry, a walled construction of rough stones of irregular size and shape.

mutule—One of a series of projecting blocks under the corona of a Doric cornice and over each triglyph, sometimes hung from the guttae.

narthex—The entry space between the front doors and the nave of a church.

nave—The larger space in a church or cathedral between the narthex and the chancel. The name is derived from the concept of the "navy" or the seating of the oarsmen of a boat or ship. Also, it is the gathering space for the parishioners for a service.

necking—The area between the lowest annulet of the capital and the astragal of the shaft of a Doric order.

oculus—A circular opening or window, often used in the wall behind the altar of a church, sometimes the narthex, frequently referred to as the "eye" at the apex of a dome.

palisade—A fence, pales or stakes set firmly in the ground for defensive purposes.

palisado—Walls made up of wood pales or stakes vertically placed in the ground, frequently configured as a fence or to support a roof for a hut, often parged over with mud or plaster to provide for domestic habitation.

parti—French term used by students of the early école de Beaux Arts, referring to the first design concept of a building or plan. Literally translated: to be among the first, proportion or part.

pediment—A low-pitched, usually triangular-shaped roof with horizontal cornices and raking cornices, frequently as an ornamental feature over windows and entrance to provide shelter. Often supported by columns, derived from the form of the Greek temple. Traditional forms include the triangular, the broken, the segmental and the scrolled.

peristyle—The range of columns and the space between the wall of a building and the columns. A row of columns forming an enclosure or supporting a roof; any space or enclosure, as a court, so formed.

pilaster—A rectangular column projecting slightly from a wall. In classical architecture it conforms with the design of the orders.

pisé—Rammed earth construction.

planking—A board, split or sawn from a timber or log, hewn on one or both sides, frequently on the edges, used to face the exterior or interior frame or log walls.

plateresque—A phase of Spanish architecture of the late-15th and early-16th centuries, an intricate style named after the likeness to silver work.

plinth—The lowest projecting member of the base of a column or pedestal, also, the projecting base, or skirt of a wall.

plinth block—A slightly projecting block at the foot of the architrave of a door, chimney piece, etc., against which the skirting is stopped. Also called an architrave block or stationary board.

portico—A covered colonnade forming an entrance to a building.

puncheon—A split log or log plank two-to-four-feet long used as floorboard in log houses, often resting loosely on the joists, occasionally pegged, more rarely resting directly on a bed of sand or dirt, containing one carefully smoothed face. Doors and shutters can also be made of purcheons.

purlin—A longitudinal member parallel to the wall but laid, usually at one third or two thirds intervals, up the slope of a roof.

quatrefoils—Each of four small arc openings in Gothic tracery, separated by cusps.

Queen Anne Style (1880-1910)—Queen Ann's reign saw the apogee of Wren and the rise of English Baroque. The term is usually applied to a development of domestic Carolean forms, principally executed in red brick. The sash window is common and hipped roofs are frequently hidden behind parapets.

quoin, coign—The external angles of a building and the rusticated or otherwise emphasized stones applied to the angles.

rack or racking—The traditional term rack is used for a structural frame. Racking in structural terminology is the deformation of a structural frame at the joint or by deflection of the members usually caused by loading conditions.

rake—The slope of a roof.

regola—The band beneath the tenia in a Doric architrave to which the cotta are attached.

retable—An altar-piece or picture, etc., behind but attached to the altar. It also refers to the shelf between the altar and the East wall.

retablo—A picture drawn on a board; a splendid ornament or altar decoration usually on the east wall behind the altar table.

Richardson Romanesque Style (1880-1900)—Identifying features include rounded arches occurring over windows, porches, or entrances; masonry walls, usually with rough-faced, squared stonework; towers which are normally round with conical roofs; and an asymmetrical façade.

rib pole—Another name for a purlin.

ridge pole—A roof support running the length of the roof ridge from one gable peak to the other. Also, the uppermost horizontal timber of a roof frame receiving the upper ends of the roof rafters.

Roman arch—A curved structure formed of wedge-shaped blocks of brick or stone (voussoirs) locked at the apex with a "keystone" and held in place by the horizontal thrust and by the vertical loads from the weight of the mass of the arch and the materials being supported above.

sacristy—An apartment or room in a church where the sacred utensils, vestments, etc. are kept; the vestry.

saddle notch—A type of log corner notching fashioned by hollowing out a saddle-shaped depression near the end, on the top, and/or on the bottom of the log. This notch is used primarily for outbuildings. It collects water and within a few years will cause the wood to decompose.

Second Empire Style (1855-1885)—Identifying features include the mansard roof with decorative dormer windows on steep sloped molded cornices normally bound the lower roof slope both above and below decorative brackets usually present beneath eaves.

shakes—Wood members used for covering roofs, usually approximately two feet long, split from a short log of cedar, white oak, cypress or other wood capable of turning water and resisting decay for an extended period. Shakes were made by splitting a section from a log approximately one-to-two-inches thick and six-to-twelve-inches wide and planing on one side to a smooth finish by a draw knife to a tapered shape.

shingles—Wood members used for roof covering, cut in a similar configuration as the shake and planed on both sides for a smooth finish.

Shingle Style (1880-1900)—Identifying features include wall cladding and roofing of continuous wood shingles without interruption at corners; asymmetrical façade with irregular, steeply pitched roof lines; intersecting gables and multi-level eaves; and exterior porches.

sill—The horizontal base of a door or window frame, the threshold of a door, the primary peripheral timber used in conventional wood framing for fastening the floor joists.

span—The horizontal distance between two supporting members, such as the abutments of an arch, or the walls carrying a roof.

spring stone—The point or support stone from which an arch rises.

square notch—A type of corner notching fashioned by removing small cube-shaped blocks of wood from both the top and bottom of the end of a log.

Stick Style (1860-1890)—Identifying features include a gabled roof, usually steeply pitched with cross gables that commonly show decorative trusses at the apex; overhanging eaves, usually with exposed rafter ends; wooden wall cladding interrupted by patterns of horizontal, vertical, or diagonal boards (stickwork) that rise from the wall surface for emphasis; and porches with diagonal braces.

stile—The extreme vertical member of a door or window frame, or in a paneled door or window shutter; the vertical member into which the horizontal rails or panels are fixed.

tenia—The uppermost fillet on a Doric architrave, separating it from the frieze.

tetrastyle portico—Portico with three supporting columns.

tiers—A rank, a range; particularly when two or more rows are placed one above another as in a "tier" of seats in an assembly room such as a church or theater.

transept—The transverse space of the cruciform church located between the nave and the chancel.

triglyph—One of the rectangular blocks between the metopes in a Doric frieze that has two vertical grooves or glyphs in the center and half-grooves on the edges, hence three grooves or "triglyph."

Tuscan order—The plainest and most massive of the five classic orders.

vault—An arched roof or ceiling, usually constructed of masonry.

veranda—An open gallery with a roof on light, usually wood, metal or masonry supports, placed along the front (and occasionally the side) of a building.

vigas—Roof beams.

volute—A spiral scroll, the distinctive feature of the Ionic capital and also used in modified form in Corinthian and Composite capitals, and in consoles and brackets.

Selected Readings and Bibliography

Abernethy, Francis Edward, ed., and Rees Kennedy, illus. *Built in Texas.* Waco: E-Heart Press, 1979.

Alexander, Drury Blakely. *Texas Homes of the Nineteenth Century.* Austin: University of Texas Press, 1966.

Allen, Carolyn, ed. *Historic Homes of San Augustine.* Austin: Encino Press in association with the San Augustine Historical Society, 1972.

Almaráz, Félix D, Jr. *The San Antonio Missions and Their System of Land Tenure.* Austin: University of Texas Press, 1989.

Almond, Killis P., Roy E. Graham, et al., eds. *Report on the Architectural Survey of Villa Guerreo, Coahuila, Mexico, and Eagle Pass, Texas, United States.* Austin: University of Texas, 1976.

Antone, Evan Haywood, ed., and Morris A. Brown, illus. *Portals at the Pass: El Paso Area Architecture to 1930.* El Paso: American Institute of Architects, 1984.

Barbee, William Clayton. "A Historical and Architectural Investigation of San Ygnacio." Master's Thesis, University of Texas at Austin, 1981.

Bolton, Herbert Eugene. *Bolton and the Spanish Border Lands.* Edited by John Francis Bannon. Norman: University of Oklahoma Press, 1964.

Brown, Angel Sepulveda, and Gloria Villa Candena. "Marriage Book I, 1790-1857." Sacramental records of the Catholic Church of San Augustine, Laredo, Texas.

Bureau of Business Research. *Atlas of Texas.* Austin: University of Texas, 1976.

Carlson, Shawn Bonath. *The Search for San Sabá: An Apache Mission on the San Sabá River, Menard County, Texas.* Archeological Survey No. 9. College Station: Texas A&M University, 1991.

Clark, John W. "Mission San José y San Miguel de Aguayo: Archaeological Investigations, December 1974." Report 29. Austin: Texas Historical Commission, 1978.

Corbin, James E. *Mission Dolores de los Ais: Archaeological Investigations of Early Spanish Colonial Missions, San Augustine County, Texas.* Nacogdoches: Stephen F. Austin State University and the Texas Antiquities Committee, 1980.

Crockett, George Louis. *Two Centuries in East Texas.* Dallas: The Southwest Press, 1932.

Crosby, H. Anthony. *Architecture of Texana, 1831-1883, Jackson County, Texas.* Palmetto Bend Reservoir Series, vol. 2, Research Report No. 57. Austin: Texas Archaeological Survey and University of Texas, 1977.

Cruz, Gilbert R. *Let There Be Towns: Spanish Municipal Origins in the American Southwest, 1610-1810.* College Station: Texas A&M University Press, 1988.

de la Peña, José Enrique. *With Santa Ana in Texas: A Personal Narrative of the Revolution.* Carmen Perry, ed. and trans. College Station: Texas A&M University Press, 1972.

DeShields, James T. *Border Wars of Texas.* . . . Tioga, Texas: Herald Company, 1912.

Eastland, Tom, and Fred Armstrong. *The Goliad Massacre.* n.p., 1974.

Ford, Powell and Carson, Architects. "The Alamo Master Plan Report for the Daughters of the Republic of Texas." San Antonio: Ford, Powell and Carson, Architects, 1979.

Foster, Nancy Haston. *The Alamo and Other Texas Missions to Remember.* Houston: Gulf Publishing Company, Lone Star Books, 1984.

Fox, Anne A., A. Feris Bass, Jr., and Thomas R. Hester. *The Archaeology and History of Alamo Plaza.* Archaeological Survey Report No. 16. Austin: University of Texas Press, 1976.

Fox, Daniel E. *Traces of History: Archaeological Evidence of the Past 450 Years.* San Antonio: Corona Publishing Company, 1983.

George, Eugene. *Historic Architecture of Texas: The Falcón Reservoir.* Austin: The Texas Historical Commission and the Texas Historical Foundation, 1975.

Gilmore, Kathleen. "Mission Rosario: Archaeological Investigations, 1973." Archaeological Report 14, Part 1. Austin: Texas Parks and Wildlife Department, 1974.

Goeldner, Paul, comp., S. Allen Chambers, Jr., and Lucy Pope Wheeler, eds. *Texas Catalog: Historic American Buildings Survey.* San Antonio: Trinity University Press, 1974.

Habig, Marion A. *Spanish Texas Pilgrimage: The Old Franciscan Missions and Other Spanish Settlements of Texas, 1632-1821.* Chicago: Franciscan Herald Press, 1990.

Hamlin, Talbot. *Greek Revival Architecture in America.* New York: Dover Publications, reproduction of the work first published by the Oxford University Press, 1944.

Harris, John and Jill Lever. *Illustrated Glossary of Architecture, 850-1830.* London: Faber and Faber, 1969.

Heimsath, Clovis. *Pioneer Texas Buildings: A Geometry Lesson.* Austin: University of Texas Press, 1968.

Hindes, V. Kay, Mark R. Wolf, Grant D. Hall, and Kathleen Kirk Gilmore. "The Rediscovery of Santa Cruz de San Sabá: A Mission for the Apache in Spanish Texas." San Sabá Regional Report 1. Texas Historical Foundation and Texas Tech University, 1995.

Johnson LeRoy, Jr., ed. *Proceedings of Texana I: The Frontier.* Austin: Texas Historical Commission, 1983.

_____. *Proceedings of Texana II: Cultural Heritage of the Plantation South.* Austin: Texas Historical Commission, 1982.

_____. *Proceedings of Texana III: The Victorian Era: Texas Comes of Age.* Austin: Texas Historical Commission, 1982.

Jordan, Terry. *Texas Log Buildings; A Folk Architecture.* Austin: University of Texas Press, 1994.

Justin, Mary Carolyn Hollers. *Alfred Giles: An English Architect in Texas and Mexico.* San Antonio: Trinity University Press, 1972.

Kimball, Fisk. *Thomas Jefferson, Architect.* Cambridge: Riverside Press, 1916.

Leutenengger, Benedict, trans. "Letters and Memorials of the Father President Fray Benito Fernández de Santa Ana, 1736-1754." San Antonio: Archives of the College of

Querétaro, Old Spanish Missions Historical Research Library at Our Lady of the Lake University.

_____ . "The San José, Papers: edited Primary Manuscript Sources for the History of Mission San José, y San Miguel de Aguayo, Part II: August 1791-June 1809." San Antonio: Old Spanish Missions Historical Research Library at San José, Mission.

_____. "Report on the Texas Missions of the College of Zacatecas, 1749-1750. Documentary Series No. 5. Recorded by Ignacio Antonio Ciprián." San Antonio: Old Spanish Missions Historical Research Library at San José, Mission.

Leutenengger, Benedict, trans., and Marion A. Habig, comp. "The San José, Papers: Primary Sources for the History of Mission San José y San Miguel de Aguayo from its founding in 1720 to the present, Part I: 1719-1791." San Antonio: Old Spanish Missions Historical Research Library at San José, Mission.

Lower Rio Grande Valley Development Council. "Historical Preservation Plan." Report No. CPA-TX-06-00-2003 (G). Brownsville, Texas: Lower Rio Grande Valley Development Council, 1978.

McCullar, Michael. *Restoring Texas: Raiford Stripling's Life and Architecture.* College Station: Texas A&M University Press, 1985.

McLemore, David. *A Place in Time: A Pictorial View of San Antonio's Past.* San Antonio: Express-News Corporation, 1980.

Meing, D. W. *Imperial Texas: An Interpretive Essay in Cultural Geography.* Austin: University of Texas Press, 1969.

Moorhead, Max L. *The Presidio: Bastion of the Spanish Borderlands.* Norman: University of Oklahoma Press, 1975.

Morrow, Herbert C. *The Mission Trail: History, Architecture, Cultural Heritage, and Historic Preservation of the Lower Valley of El Paso, Texas: A Historic Preservation Plan*. El Paso: West Texas Council of Governments and the Mission Trail Advisory Committee, 1981.

Musgrove, John, ed. *Sir Banister Fletcher's A History of Architecture*. Nineteenth Edition. London: Butterworths, 1987.

Newcomb, Rexford. *Spanish-Colonial Architecture in the United States*. New York: Dover Publications, 1990.

Noonan-Guerra, Mary Ann. *The Alamo*. San Antonio: The Alamo Press, 1983.

_____ . *The Missions of San Antonio*. San Antonio: The Alamo Press, 1982.

_____ . *San Fernando*. San Antonio: Published privately by Francis J. Furey, 1977.

_____ . *The Story of the San Antonio River*. San Antonio: The San Antonio River Authority, 1978.

O'Conner, Kathryn Stoner. *Presidio la Bahia: Espiritu Santo de Zuniga, 1721 to 1846*. Austin: Von Boeckmann-Jones Company, 1966.

Olmsted, Frederick Law. *A Journey through Texas, or, a Saddle-Trip on the Southwest Frontier*. Austin: University of Texas Press, 1978.

Robinson, Willard B. *Gone From Texas*. College Station: Texas A&M University Press, 1981.

Sánchez, Mario L., Aura Nell Ranzau, Jr., and Kitty Henderson, eds. *A Shared Experience: The Historic Designations of the Lower Rio Grande Heritage Corridor*. Austin: Los Caminos del Rio Heritage Project and the Texas Historical Commission, 1991.

Simons, Helen and Cathryn A. Hoyt. *Hispanic Texas: A Historical Guide*. Austin: University of Texas Press and Texas Historical Commission, 1992.

Simpson, Leslye Byrd. *Many Mexicos*. Berkeley: University of California Press, 1962.

South Texas Development Council. *Regional Historic Sites Survey*. Laredo, Texas: South Texas Development Council, 1979.

Steely, James Wright, comp. *A Catalog of Texas Properties in the National Register of Historic Places*. Austin: Texas Historical Commission, 1984.

Texas Historical Commission. *Hispanic Texas: A Historical Guide*. Edited by Helen Simons and Cathryn A. Hoyt. Austin: University of Texas Press, 1992.

Texas State Highway Commission. *Texas: A Guide to the Lone Star State*. Austin: Texas Monthly Press, 1986.

Tyler, Ron, et.al., eds. *The New Handbook of Texas*. Austin: The Texas State Historical Association, 1996.

Utley, Robert M., and J. U. Salvant. *If These Walls Could Talk: Historic Forts of Texas*. Austin: University of Texas Press, 1985.

Weddle, Robert S. *San Juan Bautista: Gateway to Spanish Texas*. Austin: University of Texas Press, 1988.

Index